CW01432977

BREAKING *THE* BARRIERS

EARLY INTERVENTION INTO MENTAL HEALTH ISSUES

'LADE HEPHZIBAH OLUGBEMI

2020

Breaking the Barriers
Copyright © 2020 by 'Lade Hephzibah Olugbemi

Published by
Lade Hephzibah Olugbemi Publications
lade@nousorganisation.com

ISBN 9798562688118

Printed in the EU

DISCLAIMER

This book is not intended as a substitute for the medical advice of physicians. The reader should regularly consult a physician in matters relating to his/her health and particularly with respect to any symptoms that may require diagnosis or medical attention.

Although the author and publisher have made every effort to ensure that the information in this book was correct at press time, the author and publisher do not assume and hereby disclaim any liability to any party for any loss, damage, or disruption caused by errors or omissions, whether such errors or omissions result from negligence, accident, or any other cause.

The list of symptoms and presentations should not be a self-diagnosis tool. Please ensure you always refer to your doctor for advice.

CONTENTS

DEDICATION

*This book is dedicated to the many people who have been
misunderstood, neglected, mistreated, sidestepped, or
misdiagnosed due to mental illness.
Those who have suffered the pain of stigma and shame
for an illness they sometimes did not have control over.
This book is dedicated to the many carers who have had
to care for loved ones, neighbours, children, partners,
and relatives that are diagnosed with mental illness.
To those who know the pain and the suffering of having
to conceal the shame in the community of being
stigmatised.
To those whose voices have been silenced for longed
To those who have shouted themselves hoarse asking to
be hear
This book is dedicated to the many crusaders who have
campaigned actively for a world without stigma*

ACKNOWLEDGEMENTS

There are so many people to thank and acknowledge on this journey. It is difficult to list everyone.

Thanks to the greatest muse of all, the inspirer and inspiration, the greatest activist of all who fights for equality and freedom for all, Yeshua Amasiah.

I acknowledge the support of many in this cause. When I shared the vision of the cause to start a campaign on mental health awareness in the community in 2012, it was a difficult task. I am grateful for the many organisations that gave me a platform to speak. Grateful for the many that gave the opportunity for The Nous Organisation to organise seminars and workshops in the various organisations.

I acknowledge the support and inspiration of my friend and buddy, Ms Olivia Joseph-Aluko, a great crusader for equality and advocate for equality. Her persistent encouragement for me to write this book and support is invaluable.

I want to thank and recognise the support of the many clinical support the organisation has received from our clinical friends. Dr Leah Akinlonu, our speaker at the very first seminar we organised. Additionally, recognising the support of Drs, Kalpana Dein, Femi Adebayo, Ayodele Ajayi, Tade Akintan, Shade Olajubu, Arinola Araba, Edebi Otefe, Yetunde Iriah, Maymunah Kadiri, Oyekanmi.

I recollect in 2014, my daughter had sent a message to me and it reads "Mum, you have a message and you need to shout it louder, you have the voice, go for it mum", I say thank you Rachel for inspiring and giving the clarion call to crusade. To my precious Kristina for being the critic and encourager, to Jay for accommodating support and to all of you OOM …for the the many days out in the community and allowing me to be the community champion for mental health awareness in the BAME community.

I acknowledge the support of The Nous Organisation board of directors, Ms Olivia Joseph-Aluko, Mr Paul

Chelvatheebam, Dr Shadrach Ofosuware, Mr Theo John-Philips

Acknowledging the support of the Nous Project Board in UK and Africa, members who regularly give up their time, energy and resources towards this cause – my heartfelt thanks to you to the many unpaid hours you have given to this cause.

Thank you to Cannon Yemi Adedeji for the initial brainstorming session on the concept of The Nous Organisation and the constant support to the organisation.

I thank Fuad Uddin and Charlie Fernandes for the very first job that was given the organisation to work in the London Borough of Brent to work on the Improving Access to Psychological Therapies (IAPT) programme, encouraging access to early intervention within the ethnic minority community in Brent. The various borough we have worked in London, The London Borough of Barking and Dagenham, Bexley, Royal brough of Greenwich.

Of course, to the various comrades in this crusade of being a voice for the voiceless, a mouthpiece in various places advocating for equal rights and access to services.

11

There are quite a lot more people to thank too many to mention that have pushed and encouraged against all odds. I appreciate and acknowledge you.

Please enjoy reading the book.

"If all we see are 'walls' we would be wise to remember that without a wall we would lose the privilege of building a door, or have we forgotten that that's what walls were made for."

— Craig D. Lounsbrough

The power to heal lies within us"
- 'Lade H Olugbemi

INTRODUCTION

I am 'Lade Olugbemi and I am passionate about raising awareness of mental health issues in our communities. Feel free to call me a mental health activist.

Thank you for choosing this book to read about mental health and how we as a community can break down the many barriers around mental illness that cause so many problems.

My journey into mental health conversation started back in 2008 after a personal experience.

I have heard it said that what you do not know will not hurt you... With mental health information, I have come to realise that the lack of knowledge around mental illnesses in the Black, Asian and Minority Ethnic (BAME) communities has hurt us badly. It is on record that black people are over-represented in mental health services. Higher levels of stigma and negative stereotyping are higher. So, what can we do to stop this problem? Raise awareness!

In February 2015, I started The Nous Organisation to raise levels of awareness about mental health issues. We offer peer support, advocacy and help people who have been diagnosed with mental illness or are supporting people with mental illness to make their way through the various mental health agencies.

There has been a lot of conversation about mental well-being over the last four years. Never in history have we seen such spotlight conversation on mental well-being. For a long time, mental illness has been a hushed topic and, as a result, there has been no real encouragement to discuss it openly.

The stigma against mental illness has pervaded our society like a cancer that refuses to go away, and this is a crisis of our own making. The numbers reveal why this is so. According to the World Economic Forum (WEF) and the World Health

Organization (WHO), mental health does more to drain the economy than the other various health issues.

According to WHO, one in four people in the world will be affected by mental or neurological disorders at some point in their lives. The report notes that about 450 million people currently suffer from various mental illnesses. Mental ill-health is, therefore, placed among the leading causes of ill-health and disability worldwide.

My great concern is that though treatments in the developed countries are available, nearly two-thirds of people have not been formally diagnosed and the stark truth is they may never seek help from a health professional. Stigma, discrimination, and neglect are preventing care and treatment from reaching people with mental disorders, according to the WHO. Where there is neglect, there is little or no understanding. Where there is no understanding, there is neglect.

It is scary to note that in Britain, the number of those with diagnosable mental illness who are not known to the mental health services is staggering.

Reportedly, the NHS spent around £11.2 billion between 2016 and 2017 on mental health alone. What is horrifying is that this figure was a 3.3% increase from the amount that was spent between 2015 and 2016!

Of course by deduction, the number of those who are not in contact with mental health services is higher in the ethnic minorities in developed countries, and it is worse still in developing countries – where as many as 90% of them are either never diagnosed or receive little or no form of care at all.

The reason for this is simple. It is an understandably disappointing fact that mental illness is stigmatised across the globe. People who have mental illness are tagged with labels that make them pariahs in our society. What follows is a generation that sees people with mental illness as a threat that should be neither seen nor heard.

There are several ways that the barriers around mental illness and the conversation around it can be broken. This book will discuss how this could be done.

In a sequel to this book, I will talk about my own personal experience, journey and challenges and the reason why I picked up this cause.

Of course, we recognise that the four main ways that this harmful cycle can best be broken are:

- Re-education, education, and education
- Raising awareness of the various presentations of mental ill-health
- Encouraging early intervention.

Getting to the media and stopping them from projecting mentally Ill people as being murderers or chaotic people with uncontrolled anger.

Where and when the media paints violent criminals as being mentally ill, the public will always remain confused and too scared to even want to understand what this illness is about.

Unfortunately, throughout my years as a mental health advocate, I have seen that this bias is more far-reaching than anyone might think. Besides the people who are unaware of the mentally ill or disconnected from them, there are even some professional mental health professionals who are guilty of similar stereotypes.

Mental illness does not discriminate either. Just like all types of illnesses, it does not know race, age, colour, educational achievement or status, location, profession, exposures, or shape nor size. Mental illness can happen to anyone and it permeates every socioeconomic and ethnic group, making it one of the leading causes of disability in the world. What is more worrying is that most ethnic minorities and people in developing countries do not have access to the care they need. Early intervention is not possible, so it is impossible to prevent illnesses from reaching a critical level either. Little wonder the numbers are so high. The treatment they can receive is poor at best.

> *Mental illness does not discriminate*

However, if mental health disorders were given the same level of importance as physical ailments, it would revolutionise the way they are perceived and ensure that sufferers were given timely and focused solutions to their issues, including an understanding of the role of nutrition and the benefits of natural remedies, as well as the reasons why the mentally sick are being pushed to take their own lives. Even the glitz and glamour of Hollywood cannot keep depression and anxiety at bay, no matter how much money and influence a celebrity has. Spiritual and sectarian therapy can go a long way towards helping these souls to get their lives back on track and heal from within.

This book is a clarion call to join the crusade to break down the barriers around mental illness. It is a call to recognise what the barriers are and to look at how we can pull those barriers down.

Breaking the barriers appears to be an almost insurmountable task. I recollect that 7 years ago when I started the talks in the community about mental health awareness in the Black Asian and Ethnic Minority (BAME) community, I had various challenges. The wall was very thick and extremely high. People in our community did not want to talk about mental illness and, as is common with the ethnic minority community, we prefer to bury our heads in the sands and wish that the problems will go away.

This book will not dwell majorly on the various types of mental illness. It is, instead, a journey that looks at what the barriers are, some of which are unconscious, and how we can break them.

I hope that you will enjoy reading this book and hopefully become a passionate mental well-being crusader by the time you finish reading it.

Chapter 1

WHAT IS MENTAL HEALTH?

What is Mental Health?

As previously mentioned, we will not dwell too much on this illness; however, I believe that it is important to establish what mental health is in order to understand the reason for its cause.

WHO defines health as:
"a state of complete physical, mental and social well-being and not merely the absence of disease or infirmity."

And mental health is:
"... a state of well-being in which the individual realizes his or her own abilities, can cope with the normal stresses of life, can work productively and fruitfully, and is able to make a contribution to his or her community".

The state of our mental health determines how we think and how we feel about ourselves and others. It affects our perspective about how we interpret situations and how we can process thoughts, as well as our abilities to sustain relationships and cope with life changes and events.

Mental health is a continuum; it is not static, but a journey, and we all move on the spectrum of mental health. People can move from having good mental health to having poor mental health. A person can have poor mental health without a mental health diagnosis and a person with a mental health diagnosis can have good mental health.

The state of our mental health determines how we think and how we feel about ourselves

According to WHO, your ability and capacity to cope when there is a life stressor determines whether you have good mental health or not.

There are different words that people have used to define mental illness. In fact, language is one of the challenges and barriers to mental illness in our community – the language that we use to describe this illness. The media has not helped the matter as their use of negative descriptions of the condition have only perpetuated the negative impression that people have of mental health.

Some of the words used to describe mental illness are:

- mental illness
- mental distress
- mental disorder
- mental health problem
- mental health difficulties
- mental health issues
- mental health challenge
- emotional disorder
- nervous breakdown
- mental breakdown
- burnout

I am certain that if I was to start to list the negative words used to describe mental health, it would be endless – crazy, psycho, schizo, looney, nuts, crackhead, wacko, gone with the fairies, mad – to name but a few.

When a person is mentally ill, it means their thinking, perception, emotions, and behaviour affect how they behave and think, as well as their ability to work and carry out daily activities.

It is a psychiatric disorder that affects the behavioural or **mental** pattern of the person and causes significant distress or impairs a person's ability to function.

Chapter 2

FACTORS THAT CAUSE STIGMA AGAINST MENTAL ILLNESS

The World Health Organisation (WHO) recognises that: *"The single most important barrier to overcome in the community is the stigma and associated discrimination towards persons suffering from mental and behavioural disorders."*

So, what causes the stigma? Why do we in the community look at a person who may not have it all together in their mind and deem them to be mentally 'unfit'?

Stigma is defined as "a mark of disgrace associated with a particular circumstance, quality, or person". It is a set of negative, unpleasant, and often unfair beliefs and actions that a society or group of people have about something. Stigma against mental illness occurs when someone, or even yourself, views a person negatively just because they have a mental health condition. Some people describe stigma as a feeling of shame or judgement from someone else.

There are two main types of stigma that occur with mental health problems:
- social stigma
- self-stigma

Social stigma, or public stigma, refers to negative stereotypes of those with a mental health problem. These stereotypes come to define the person, mark them out as different and prevent them from being an individual.

Self-Stigma can even come from an internal place, as a person can stigmatise themselves. This is when you confuse *feeling* bad with *being* bad.

Navigating life with a mental health condition can be tough, and the isolation, blame and secrecy that is often encouraged by stigma can create huge challenges that stop people from reaching out, getting much-needed support and living well. Learning how to both avoid and address stigma are important for all of us, especially when you realise stigma's effects.

Historically speaking, humanity has always been wary of people who look, act or think differently. Since fear begets violence, the mentally ill have been treated poorly, if not out and out brutalised by the mentally fit for decades.

What is astonishing is that this compulsion stems from the view that people with mental illness are unpredictably violent. The early beliefs in several cultures were that mental illness was caused by demonic possession or the occult which naturally led to fear and ultimately, stigmatisation. People who hold such thoughts sometimes believe that these demons can transfer to another person, so they avoid people with mental illness altogether.

Astonishingly, these superstitions are also present in the medical profession, which should be acting as a bulwark against such prejudice. Medical professionals do this by comparing mental health issues with physical ailments, even though many of them find it challenging to diagnose with any certainty.

It comes down to the difference between mental health and mental illness. The former refers to our emotional and psychological state – how we feel about ourselves or our social well-being and how we interact with others. Plus, while poor mental health can lead to physical ailments, these effects can be curbed by physical activity or medical intervention. Mental illness, on the other hand, refers to illnesses that affect behaviour. The type and severity of the illness determine the way that those afflicted with a mental illness interact with the world around them. Unfortunately, most medical services view mental illness as poor mental health and try to treat it as such.

I know that in mental health activism, we often discuss how much of a problem stigma is and how much it impacts those who live with mental illness. Stigma harms 1 in 5 people affected by mental health issues. Stigma shames and forces people into silence and prevents them from seeking help early. We do need to talk about the foundation of what causes stigma and that is one of the reasons that I have written this book.

Several studies show that stigma usually arises from a lack of awareness, lack of education, lack of perception, and the nature and complications of mental illness. For example, odd behaviours and violence, as well as the fear of being infected or affected.

Think about it. If you break an arm, you know it can be fixed with a cast or a simple surgery. A mental illness such as depression, which may originate from childhood trauma or a multitude of traumatic incidents, cannot be fixed with a simple patch job. Medication may numb the pain for a while, but if it stops working, there is no cast to fix that damage.

It is not strange that three out of four people with a mental illness report that they have experienced stigma. When a person is labelled by their illness they are no longer

Stigma drives stereotyping, stereotyping drives prejudice, and prejudice drives discrimination.

seen as an individual but as part of a stereotyped group. Negative attitudes and beliefs toward this group create prejudice which leads to negative actions and discrimination.

Stigma drives *stereotyping, stereotyping* drives *prejudice,* and prejudice drives *discrimination.*

- The impact of stigma is immense and includes:
- Experiences and feelings of shame
- Blame, hopelessness, distress
- Secrecy, loneliness, isolation, and social exclusion
- Stereotyping and derogatory labels
- Misrepresentation by the media
- Being treated differently than the rest of society
- Discrimination in housing, employment, and services

Stigma worsens a person's illness and can lead to a reluctance to seek and/or accept necessary help. It is not just the person who is affected; the families are also affected by stigma, leading to a lack of disclosure and support.

Interestingly, this negative stereotype extends to people who work as mental health professionals. Therefore, the professionals themselves are sometimes seen as being abnormal, corrupt, or evil, and are, in some cultures, viewed with suspicion and horror.

We ought to drive for a greater understanding of mental ill health. This is necessary and until we change our language, our understanding will always be limited

Language

Language provides the active ingredients that perpetuates stigma in our communities and this is one of the major barriers that we have to break!

The various languages that we use to describe or not to describe mental ill health is very negative, discriminatory and they exclude the person with mental illness. The languages used are systemic and people have grown up hearing such lexicons like; psycho, schizo, mad, crazy, Yaba left, Skoin skoin, insane, mental, OCD, committed suicide etc.

We have to change the narrative about the descriptors for mental ill health. The negative labelling of mental illness has permeated our society and there is a need to start a crusade to challenge this. Negative words are a major barrier to people admitting that they have mental ill health. No one wants to be described as 'mad' 'psycho' or schizo, so it will be challenging for anyone to want to own up to hearing voices or seeing images no one else is seeing.

Swapping these negative words can help to start the ending of the stigma. We all need to realise that the choices of our words contribute to the stigma, the marginalisation of persons with mental ill health.

Evidence shows that we all respond to words. When we hear some words, some feelings are evoked. A word brings an idea, a feeling and in turn, an idea triggers many other ideas and emotions and reactions. We often react to words without realising it.

I believe that if we understood the import and the effects of words and the triggers in our brains and the reactions, perhaps we will all be a lot more careful with the words we use to describe mental ill health.

I am a student of languages and also understand that words evolve and that with conscious effort, awareness and education we can change the use of these negative descriptors. Once upon a time, 'psychotic' 'neurotic' were common words used to describe mental ill health, thankfully these words are not commonly used now. Hopefully the use of such words as 'nutter' crazy' will become a thing of the past.

As part of my work as a Mental Health First Aid Instructor, one of the messages I pass on to delegates is the way we describe when a person takes their own life, we often say the person 'committed suicide'. The use of the word, 'commit' makes it look like the person committed a crime or they have performed an unlawful act. This denotation may be down to historic facts where and when suicide was deemed as a sin and a crime. **The Suicide Act 1961** decriminalised the act of suicide in England and Wales so that those who failed in the attempt to kill themselves would no longer be prosecuted. Therefore, it is important to note that suicide is not a crime in the England and Wales albeit still a crime in Scotland and the other 3 countries. When we look at the impact of suicide on the comunity, family members, colleagues, we should be a lot more careful in how we describe suicide. Expressions

We must realise that our languages and communications styles can be emotionally charged and can be responsible for our actions. How we talk and describe mental ill health matters.

The charge to all of us in the community is to be a lot more thoughtful about how we talk especially when we think of the fact that there is a likelihood that 1 in 6 of us will experience mental health issues in our lifetime. How we all talk and describe mental ill health in our environment matters.

How would you want to be treated if you are 1 of the 6?

Media

The past 10 years has seen an exponential increase in the use of media technology. The tablets, smartphones, laptops, blogs, text messaging, whatsapps, Facebook, Instagram, messenger video rooms have helped in connecting with businesses, families and communities.

There has been a decrease in the use of the traditional sources of mass media, like Television, newspaper, radio and books. The truth like we all should know is that mass media has a powerful effect on our way of life, our values, beliefs, our expectations, the food we eat, clothes we wear and how we basically live our lives. The influence of mass media is immense, pervasive and intrusive.

The effects of mass media are both positive and negative and it does drive perceptions and it shapes behaviours. The media has been known to play a key role in misconceptions and has at the same time helped to build concepts. Media have played a role in breaking down misconceptions and myths about homosexuality, leprosy, and HIV/AIDS. It is hoped that it can do the same for mental illness and various psychiatric disorders.

The media has continued to contribute to the stigma about mental illness. This is done through the many times that they have exaggerated the illness and painted inaccurate, and comical images in portraying persons with mental illness as well as providing incorrect information.

Since most people have not had a lived experience on mental illness, people end up relying on the media for their perceptions of those who have mental illnesses. Unfortunately, the media consistently portrays persons with mental illness as violent, disjointed, argumentative, dangerous, unpredictable and they are blamed for their conditions. Most times there are gross exaggerations and misrepresentations of reality and completely untrue.

This has created a major barrier in people having better understanding of what mental illness is and has resulted in the belief in the general population that persons with psychiatric disorders are uncontrollable and dangerous and should be feared and avoided.

The print media scream over sensationalist headlines with dramatic language describing violent attacks and murders committed by persons with psychiatric illnesses.The media do not make it clear to the public, however, that only a minority of those with mental illness commit severe crimes and that the actual occurrence of violence by persons with mental illness is less than by so-called normal people. Oftentimes the reverse is the case, persons with mental illness are often victims of abuse, violence and killed.

The same tool used to create the barrier should be used to break the barrier of stigma.

The media can do this by ensuring that their

reports are good and responsible with accurate and balanced facts of events. They should be helping the community to understand what mental illnesses are by including the perspective of people with mental illness, carers, and mental health workers and encourage early intervention.

The media should consider in the reports;

Normalise Mental Illness

- The same way it is 'normal' to have a headache when stressed. The same way a bone may be broken in an accident, that same way, a person can have mental illness if they are unable to cope with stressors of life. Mental illness is real. Normalise it and let people know that it is TREATABLE!
- Feature stories about people with a mental illness playing an active role in the community.

- Emphasize the impact that mental illness has on family members, friends, and carers.

Promote HOPE

- The media must give hope to this dark topic. Showcase stories about the successful management of mental illness by featuring people who have recovered and are holding down good jobs. This is not to downplay the illness but also to spotlight the challenges and raise awareness about managing the illness.

Promote Early Intervention

- The media should use the platforms to encourage people who show symptoms of mental illness to seek for help

- Emphasis must be laid on recognition of the illness and treatment. Raise awareness about mental health services and encourage people in distress not to delay seeking help.

Promote Information

- Promote and provide accurate information about psychiatric disorders from reliable resource sources. Mental illness, like some other illnesses, is complex and this should be highlighted. It should be emphasised that mental illness covers a wide range of symptoms, conditions, and effects on people's lives, but most of them improve with treatment.

Promote the use of right Language

- The media should lead in the effort to ensure the use of appropriate language. Negative terms, such as "psycho", "mental patient," "nutter," "lunatic,", "insane" "psycho," "schizo" and "mental institution," should be avoided. Such words encourage stigma and perpetuates discrimination. Referring to someone with a mental illness as a "psycho," "madman" or "afflicted by" a mental illness is negative.

- Refrain from the use of describing people by their diagnosis such as, she is "Bipolar", or "a schizophrenic;". The positive way to put it is, "they have a diagnosis of...", "currently experiencing", or are "being treated for the disorder".

- Avoid using colloquialisms in place of accurate terminology for treatments of mental illness, such as "happy pills" for antidepressants and "shrinks" to refer to psychiatrists. It trivialises the illness and its treatment and may discourage persons from continuing treatment

Apart from the media, We should refrain from using mental disorders to describe everyday activities for example;

Describing an everyday mood swing as a person having Bipolar Disorder

- Describing an organised and tidy person as having OCD - Obsessive Compulsive Disorder
- Describing feelings of sadness and saying "I am depressed" or "that is depressing". Feeling sad is not the same as living with depression.
- Using coinages used to describe person with mental illness to describe someone we do not like

Culture and Religion

One of the barriers to early intervention is the culture, beliefs and religion of communities. The impact of culture on our attitude to mental illness and the stigma surrounding does count! Mental illness is considered the product of a complex interaction among biological, psychological, social, and cultural factors. The impact of one or all of this can be stronger or weaker depending on the diagnosis.

Cultural Perspectives on Mental Illness. Attitudes toward mental illness vary among individuals, families, ethnicities, cultures, and countries. Cultural and religious teachings often influence beliefs about the origins and nature of mental illness, and shape attitudes towards the persons with mentally ill health.

Our collective thoughts create consciousness in society's culture and also impacts on the beliefs, norms and values. It impacts how you view certain ideas or behaviors. And in the case of mental health, it can impact whether or not you seek help, what type of help you seek and what support you have around you can affect the readiness and willingness to seek and adhere to treatment.

Therefore, understanding individual and cultural beliefs about mental illness is essential for putting strategies and structures in place to break any barriers and institute effective approaches to mental health care.

Cultural beliefs towards mental illness differ from community to community. For instance, while some cultures do not stigmatise mental illness, others stigmatise only some types of mental illnesses, and other tribes stigmatise all mental illnesses.

In most Asian cultures, high value is placed on conforming to norms, emotional self-control, and family honor through achievement, mental illnesses are highly stigmatised and seen as a source of shame. However, the stigmatisation of mental illness can be influenced by other factors, such as the perceived cause of the illness.

This is one of the major barriers that community leaders, governmental structures have to challenge and break

In a 2003 study, Chinese Americans and European Americans were presented with a vignette in which an individual was diagnosed with schizophrenia or a major depressive disorder. Participants were then told that experts had concluded that the individual's illness was "genetic", "partly genetic", or "not genetic" in origin, and participants were asked to rate how they would feel if one of their children dated, married, or reproduced with the subject of the vignette. Genetic attribution of mental illness significantly reduced unwillingness to marry and reproduce among Chinese Americans, but it increased the same measures among European Americans, supporting previous findings of cultural variations in patterns of mental illness stigmatization.

There is also a culture of negative attitude toward health care professionals among those who work in the mental health sector. Many African countries harbour great distrust for these professionals and often label them as having mental health illness too. The cultural attitude is that since they spend most of the time at work they very likely will have 'picked up mental illness' too.

In 2007, a study was done in America by The National Mental Health Association reporting that approximately 63% of African Americans viewed depression as a "personal weakness", 30% reported that they would deal with depression themselves, and only one-third reported that they would accept medication for depression if prescribed by a medical professional.

These cultural barriers create such great stigma that it makes people less likely to receive proper diagnosis and treatment for depression or any other mental illness which means they are more likely to have the illness for longer periods.

Religious and cultural beliefs may discourage many people from seeking treatment for depression and other mental health disorders. Religious faith is an important source of strength for people who experience stress and mental illness,

There are still many religions that believe that mental illness is caused by sin or a lack of faith or that it can be cured by prayer alone. With such belief, the likelihood of people seeking help early is slim and this will add to their suffering.

I recollect growing up in Africa with and observing how mentally ill people were ostracized and where families that had family members with the illness refusing to talk about it and in some extreme cases they were locked up in rooms.

From the 6 years experience I have had in the community delivering seminars and speaking at various faith events, I have spoken to many that were diagnosed with depression and other disorders, and they have expressed that they have been accused by their faith leaders and brethren that their illnesses was caused by a lack of faith or prayer or that they were under, the influence of evil spirits or a they were under a curse.

The fear of being deemed as weak in faith, unstable or demonised is a major barrier to people seeking help early. This is one of the barriers that has to be broken.

The BAME communities are very religious and the influence that religious leaders wield is very strong. It is very important to recognise that one of the key areas to look into in breaking this barrier is culture and religion. Government and organisations should engage the voluntary sector in engaging with faith-based organisations and other community venues to help them address the stigma associated with mental illness

In conclusion, we recognise the fact that stigma against people with mental illnesses has increased over the past half century and is still increasing. So many studies have also shown that the major cause of this stigma is the perception that some individuals with mental illnesses are dangerous, the languages we use to describe mental illness, culture and religion. Of course the list highlighted above is not exhaustive. There are also other stigma drivers like; educational status, poverty, age and race.

We all can help in the campaign to break the barrier around the stigma against people with mental illness. We must all remember that the stigma makes it difficult for people to seek help early and also make it more difficult to recover.

Chapter 3

FACTORS THAT MAY CAUSE MENTAL ILLNESS

To talk effectively about the barriers that we need to break around discussing mental health issues, we also need to understand this illness. It is necessary for us to understand some elements of mental illness. I have found out that one of the driving forces behind stigma is the fact that people find it easier to pack to the side, a phenomenon they are not familiar with. It becomes so much easier for people to run away from the knowledge that culture and tradition has told them it should be shrouded and only very few people should understand it.

Ignorance of what mental illness is one of the major barriers that we have to break and so we will need to mention some of the few factors.

What Causes Mental Illness?

There are various factors that affect people and can trigger off mental unwellness.

Life is in phases and seasons. Life comes with its peaks and troughs. We all go through difficult times and we all react differently to those difficult times. Our capacity and reactions during the tough times is determined by many factors. With some their reactions can be a healthy reaction to feel negative emotions when facing challenges in our lives and some it can be an unhealthy reaction. There is no right or wrong way to react to a situation.

Life affects us all differently, but certain factors can affect our mental health and influence how we think and respond to challenges and opportunities in life.

Being aware of how challenges in life can affect our mental health may make it easier to understand when we, or someone we care about, are struggling.

There are various causes of mental illness. It is important to note some causes of mental illness are complex and varying depending on the particular type of diagnosis and the person. Also, the factors causing mental ill health are not fully understood, researchers have identified a variety of biological, psychological, and environmental factors that can contribute to the development or progression of mental disorders. Most mental ill health are a result of a combination of several different factors rather than just a single factor

The factors listed below are not exhaustive however are among the most common triggers:

Genetics

• Biological factors can be anything physical that can cause adverse effects on a person's mental health. This includes genetics, prenatal damage, infections, exposure to toxins, brain defects or injuries, and substance abuse.

Environmental Factors

• Several environmental factors, like loneliness or a stressful life event, can cause mental illness. A person is predisposed and has a higher chance of developing mental illness and also reacts negatively to a life stressor where a person has a family history of mental illness

- Bringing and environment
- Life experiences
- Self-esteem. This is the value we place on ourselves, our positive self-image and sense of self-worth
- Family breakup or loss
- Difficult behaviour
- Physical ill health
- Sexual, emotional, physical abuse
- Childhood abuse, trauma, or neglect
- Social isolation or loneliness - living on your own
- Experiencing discrimination and stigma
- Racism and bullying
- Social isolation and disadvantage
- Poverty or debt
- Bereavement - death of a spouse, family member, partner or friend
- Severe or long-term stress
- Relocation
- Poor family connection
- Difficulties socialising and feeling like you don't belong

As mentioned earlier the list of the triggers is not exhaustive and also the fact that some of the triggers are combined.

I would like to look at some of the factors

Loneliness

The Oxford Dictionary defines Loneliness as *"feelings of sadness because one has no friends or company, or "feelings of depression and loneliness"*.

To help us understand this better we will look at some of the synonyms for Loneliness: Isolation, friendlessness, lack of friends/companions, abandonment, rejection, unpopularity

It can also be defined as feeling sad about being by yourself, particularly over a long period of time. Isolation is being separated from other people and your environment. Loneliness can sometimes be felt even when a person is in relationships or when surrounded by people.

Loneliness can trigger mental health issues. When a person is isolated from contact with people or they may be in a crowd and are too connected, this can have a negative impact on mental well being. Please note that this feeling of loneliness we describe here is not the same as the normal feeling that one experiences at some time in their lives when they miss someone, those feelings are normal and usually pass but if they don't go away and last for a long time, it can have a negative impact on your mental health and wellbeing.

There are many reasons why people feel lonely or isolated. Some reasons may include:
- Bereavement
- Poor family relationship
- Social phobia
- Poor physical health
- Mental health issues or conditions

It is important to note that when you get these feelings you should not give up and move away from people.

- Stay connected. Positive friends and families are a great protective factor and they can make a difference to how you feel. Seemingly little effort like catching up with family or friends you may have lost touch with. You should not always wait for them to make the first move, you can too.

- Stay connected in the community. Resist the urge to want to stay at home . If you are able to go out, go out visiting, exercise, volunteer.

Bullying

Bullying is often not recognised as a trigger for mental health issues. The deliberate act of hurting, upsetting, threatening, repeatedly and intentionally subjecting someone to verbal, physical and/or social behaviour that causes physical and/or psychological harm is bullying.

The impact of this behavior on the victim can go unrecognised and in such cases little attention or support is offered.

Recent report on Stopbullying.gov.uk reports that 20% of students ages 12 to 18 stated that they have experienced bullying. 30% of young people admit that they have also bullied others.And sadly, the impact of bullying on these young people is that they are more at risk of suicidal thoughts, sleeping difficulties, poor performance in school, self harm, anxiety and eating disorders, post traumatic disorders and depression.

The most common form of bullying amongst young people is cyberbullying.

Workplace bullying is another form of bullying

that is the display of unreasonable behaviour, sometimes covert, directed at a colleague that creates a health and safety issue to the worker.

Whether overt or covert, whatever the format of the bullying, everyone's experience is different and it can affect every part of their life including their mental health and wellbeing. Most people who have experienced bullying mention the feeling of powerlessness, desecrated and violated. They sometimes find it difficult to talk about what is happening can become more and more isolated, which may lead to an increased risk of experiencing mental health issues.

For anyone going through bullying, you need to take action. The barrier has to be broken. Staying quiet and not stopping the bullying allows the perpetrator to continue. Albeit, whilst challenging, it is important to look after yourself and get support.

- The following tips may help:
- ask them to stop
- walk away and don't respond to them
- talk to someone
- keep a diary

- report the bullying
- get support from friends, family or someone you trust

Insomnia - Sleeping difficulties

Insomnia is having sleeplessness. Sleep is essential and a good night sleep is essential to our mental and physical health and wellbeing. Our bodies repair itself when we sleep and when there is a lack of sleep, it can have a major impact on our mood, concentration, memory and quality of life. Lack of sleep can also make us physically unwell and scientists have reported that lack of sleep contributes to heart diseases and premature aging.

Good quality sleep is about the amount of 'deep sleep' a person gets, not the length of sleep. However with the increasingly busy lives we all live now, it is estimated that we now sleep around 90 minutes less each night than we did in previous decades. A lot of us are permanently sleep-deprived.

There are some good tips to good sleep;
- Develop a regular sleep pattern or timing
- Exercise regularly - avoid exercises 3 hours before your bedtime

- Use the bed for sleep only - avoid taking your laptops or mobile devices to bed
- Spend some time unwinding before going to bed
- Avoid alcohol, caffeine, nicotine - particularly before bed
- Play music, hot bath or shower and make your bedroom and bed comfortable
- Get professional help is you experience sleeplessness for over 2 weeks

Substance Abuse - Alcohol And Other Drug Use
Alcohol, caffeine and other substances are sometimes used by people to cope during difficult times in life. A big caution must be observed as there is a strong link between alcohol and other drug use and mental health issues.

Alcohol, cannabis and other drug uses can also cause anxiety, depression, paranoia and psychosis in those people who have a vulnerability to mental health issues.

Alcohol and other drug use influences the way people behave, feel and decision making. Whilst someone may use alcohol or other drugs because they think it makes them feel better in the short-term, the long term effect actually can leave you feeling worse, especially if the person already has an existing mental health issue.

Please note that alcohol and other drug use can trigger off mental health issues in many ways including:

- Affecting self esteem
- Increasing suicidal thoughts
- Likelihood of self harming, if there are underlying issues
- Affecting your mood in the longer term
- Impacting on other coping skills
- Affecting relationships

Substance abuse and alcohol are barriers to early intervention and prevention and we have to watch out for its effect and impacts on our mental health.

Migration

Many migrants face difficulty acclimating to a new lifestyle, culture, language, and people who don't understand their values. Most people migrate to provide a better future for themselves and their family members, not realizing the trauma that awaits them before they can settle. Many are not mentally prepared for settlement.

Stress is the natural outcome along with a series of powerful emotions such as anxiety and depression. The result is often Post Traumatic Stress Disorder which can compromise their quality of life further and make acclimatization challenging to say the least.

Unresolved Trauma

Unresolved trauma is also one of the main causes behind several mental illnesses. It can haunt us throughout our lives in ways that may not seem direct. Glossing over the past does nothing but make the effects of the trauma fester till the boil erupts so to speak. Old wounds may trigger involuntary reactions that an individual may have buried for years such as guilt, fear, shame, or anger among others.

Trauma is often the result of overwhelming negative events and emotions, and it can have lasting effects on mental stability. While most causes of trauma are physical in nature (such as rape, domestic abuse, or severe illness or injuries), others are psychological. For example, a person can be traumatized if he/she witnesses a violent incident.

When we don't deal with trauma, we tend to carry it with us for the rest of our lives. Even if the memory of the trauma is repressed, it can crop up without warning. This can be in the form of:

- Anxiety attacks triggered under normal situations.
- Feelings of shame or worthlessness.
- Ongoing depression.
- Avoidance of people, locations, and things that remind them of the traumatic event. It can also lead to an avoidance of certain unpleasant emotions.
- Nightmares, unpleasant flashbacks, and tendencies regarding the traumatic incident.
- Substance abuse and eating disorders that help them gloss over negative emotions.
- Insomnia and other sleeping issues.
- Feelings of detachment from the world and people leading to isolation and loneliness.
- Suicidal thoughts and tendencies.
- Constantly being on guard.
- Inability to tolerate arguments or any conflict.
- Uncontrollable anger.

Poverty and Homelessness

To understand mental health and poverty, we have to understand that the latter involves more than a lack of income. It can also come about if individuals are prevented from accessing services and goods that can help them improve their quality of life. This includes employment, decent wages, safe neighbourhoods complete with public amenities, and basic human rights as well.

Besides this, people who suffer from serious mental health issues face a number of obstacles when it comes to their survival and their access to a nurturing lifestyle. Many individuals face obstacles when they try to get a decent education and employment that can help them survive. Unfortunately, due to stigma and discrimination against the mentally ill, many face limited employment and educational opportunities which in turn affects their ability to earn a suitable income.

In addition, individuals who suffer from mental health issues also face discrimination when it comes to accessing community services and support. If they do have access to these services, they usually have to contend with complex systems and gaps in service that seriously impede their recovery and/or treatment.

With a lack of sufficient primary care and community mental health aid, insufficient income support, and a serious shortage of affordable housing, many poverty-stricken mentally ill individuals find themselves destitute and alone. Lack of social support results in isolation and increases the risk of homelessness.

However, the connection between mental illness and homelessness is not based on a cause and effect relationship. That's because there are a number of issues that work to cause both, so we cannot say that the former causes the latter or vice versa.

We can say that poor mental health can lead to homelessness when the symptoms become severe enough to prevent the individual from leading a normal life or prevent him/her from functioning. Depending on the ailment they are suffering from, they may be disorganized or unable to hold down a paying job.

Certain neurological ailments such as bipolar disorder and schizophrenia not only make employment impossible, but these also prevent individuals from taking care of themselves. This leads to isolation which is often involuntary – many people who suffer from emotional imbalances are abandoned by their families since there is a serious lack of awareness regarding their care.

On the contrary, homelessness can also cause mental illnesses due to the trauma that can result from living on the streets. The trauma can also lead to post traumatic stress disorder (PTSD) and depression especially in individuals who are susceptible to mental ailments due to genetic or environmental factors.

The list of the triggers and causes of mental ill health we have given above is not exhaustive; they have been highlighted to give us a guide in recognising that these triggers need to be recognised and avoided where possible.

Chapter 4
THE MEDIA AND MENTAL ILLNESS

By the media, we mean any channel of communication where information is disseminated, including newspapers, social media platforms, educational content, and numerous other forms of information.

How do we explain it? The increase in the number of people diagnosed with anxiety disorders, the higher number of people who report that they are lonely.

The push to get on social media is difficult to resist. Fear of Missing Out (FOMO) has turned many people into social media junkies. Of course, we cannot help but agree that social media has an impact on mental health.

The rapid growth of social media over the last decade has established an entirely new medium of human interaction. Online platforms such as Facebook, LinkedIn, Snapchat, Twitter, and Instagram have allowed people in every corner of the world to be connected 24/7.

By 2021, it is forecast that there will be around 3 billion active monthly users of social media. From the statistics alone, it is clear that social media has become an integral (and to a large extent, unavoidable) part of our lives. One implication of social media's rapid rise is that its relationship with people's mental health has gathered a significant amount of attention in recent years. There is a wide range of evidence that confirms the link between social media use and mental health.

Furthermore, there is emerging evidence social media's popularity as a medium of communication for young people needs to be carefully examined, as it may indeed come to play a more detrimental role than we first thought.

So-called 'social media addiction' has been referred to by a wide variety of studies and experiments. It is thought that addiction to social media affects around 5% of young people and was recently described as potentially more addictive than alcohol and cigarettes.

Social media's negative impact and its 'addictive' nature are largely due to the degree of the compulsive way we use it. The 'urge' to check one's social media may be linked to both instant gratification (the need to experience fast, short-term pleasure) and dopamine production (the chemical in the brain associates with reward and pleasure). We have gradually caved into the desire for a 'hit' of dopamine that we get when we reach for our phones.

The emotional tie is so difficult as it is coupled with a failure when you don't get this kick of instant gratification, which means you are prompted to perpetually refresh your social media feeds.

So, do not believe everything you see on social media. Do not compare your life with everyone you see on social media; the pictures have been filtered and mirages.

The influence that social media and the media generally has on the perception of mental illness further exacerbates the perception of how people with mental illness are perceived.

What society fails to understand about mental illness, the media exacerbates. In fact, what we see and hear on television is largely responsible for how we perceive people with mental illness. Most portrayals are quite negative, insignificant and inaccurate, even if the portrayal is considered to be 'positive.' The misunderstandings that can stem from such misrepresentations often result in consequences that are harmful, not only for such individuals, but also public perception.

Take inaccurate representations of schizophrenia, for example. It is often falsely labelled as a personality disorder, which has led to several wrong beliefs, not to mention conflicts that have led to a delay in treatments. Due to these misconceptions, the mentally ill continue to be on the receiving end of negativity just because of the amount of prejudice and fear there is. This is one of the main reasons why they are unloved, forgotten and shoved to the fringes of society. In fact, they are written off, courtesy of the wrong media misrepresentation. The fact is that our prejudices and our understanding of mental illness are sometimes influenced by the media. When we look at how McMurphy was presented in the film, *One Flew Over the Cuckoo's Nest*, it is clear that our impression of Electroconvulsive Therapy (ECT) was distorted by the movie's image of the procedure.

According to Mind, a UK-based charity on mental health, media coverage of the mentally ill is so negative that it has a direct and harmful impact on their lives. The charity came to this conclusion after it surveyed more than 500 people who had suffered from a range of mental health issues regarding their views on such media coverage.

According to the survey, half of the respondents revealed that the negative media coverage made them feel isolated, withdrawn and more misunderstood than before. Many of them also revealed that it made them feel more anxious and depressed while others said they felt suicidal after watching the media coverage.

In addition, almost 25% of them revealed that they felt hostility from neighbours who had seen reports and negative coverage on the television and in newspapers. Almost 10% of respondents reported that they had to seek mental health aid after seeing the same coverage and 25% said that they could not bring themselves to apply for jobs because of this.

In other words, the media's misguided and unjust depiction not only reduces the chances of their recovery, it also encourages prejudice and violence against them. This, in turn, creates barriers that prevent the mentally ill from finding decent employment, housing and educational opportunities. In other words, the effects of this stigma can create an extra burden for people who already live in their own personal hell.

It is horrifying to know the extent that films, newspapers, television, and social media platforms influence our perceptions. The experiences of people with mental illness influence us less. I have worked with people with depression, anxiety disorders, schizophrenia, bipolar and they are regular people like you and me. People with mental illness are negatively portrayed by the media as violent, and they are not. The interesting thing is that if you asked someone where their perception was derived from, they would probably tell you that it was from what they were told or read.

Reading the newspaper can bring about a whole new set of complications. We know that bad news sells faster, so I suppose the media platforms, both electronic and print, use screaming negative headlines to sell. Equally, for journalists with a deadline who need a good story, the more negative the story, the more eyeballs, or hearers there will be. I think it delights journalists to dig into the past of offenders and they sometimes erroneously imply that mental illness has some effect on the offending behaviour.

According to the Canadian Mental Health Association "... *as a group, people with mental health issues are not more violent than any other group in our society. The majority of crimes are not committed by people with psychiatric illness, and multiple studies have proven that there is very little relationship between most of these diseases and violence*".

The misconception is further worsened by how mental illness is exaggerated by the media when a violent or tragic event happens. We have seen instances when there has been a terrorist attack or a school shooting, and the perpetrator's mental illness is portrayed as being a dark and lurking trigger.

Psychiatrists and psychotherapists have been depicted as inefficient, incompetent people who do not exercise due duty of care to the patients by letting them out of the ward early or not increasing their medication dosages.

When people with mental illness face barriers that prevent them from acquiring amenities, it invariably decreases their chances of survival. When the illness affects the person's ability to work, there are not enough alternative activities to engage the mind and they may sometimes just end up wandering around homeless, jobless, and destitute. This only decreases their chances of acquiring timely medical aid and intervention that is often necessary in case they try to hurt themselves.

Unfortunately, due to the stigma and negative portrayal of mental illness (that is exacerbated by the media), these individuals also have difficulty acquiring the education they need to get decent jobs. The recurrence of their symptoms is often the reasons cited for their inability to acquire a steady income that can help them pay for the help they need. In other words, insufficient income, a lack of education, including access to higher education, coupled with the stigma surrounding their condition, contribute to their exclusion from society. The result is chronic poverty that, ironically, can only be alleviated if they are allowed access to those things.

That is not to say the prejudice is completely deliberate. The stigma that is attached to mental disorders today stems from biases that date back centuries. Think of the fear of such individuals as an insatiable monster that feeds on negativity. Negative media images are responsible for encouraging this attitude which continues to feed off each inaccurate fact.

The narrative can be changed, however. The same tool that spreads the negativity can be used to propagate the change. The media should take it upon themselves to be a tool to cause positive change.

The recommendations are the drive for the change that is required and should be engineered by people with lived experience. The rudder of this great change should be given to mental health advocates and carers.

Positive, repetitive and accurate depictions of people who are struggling with unseen 'demons' have to become commonplace before perceptions can change for the better.

We have seen films that portray mental illness properly. Scriptwriters have done their research well and therefore written authentic lines, and producers have produced scenes that are like how the symptoms and presentations can be in real life.

An example is the film series, **Homeland**. This Netflix film is about spies and espionage activities. Carrie Mathison is the central character who lives with bipolar disorder. Hannah Parkinson of The Guardian Newspapers UK, who lives with Bipolar Disorder, surmises that the portrayal of Carrie Mathison's bipolar disorder is refreshingly accurate. In the fourth season, Carrie's mental illness becomes the central plot. Carrie, the main character, is exceptionally intelligent and living with bipolar disorder. The depiction of the manic episodes is usually characterised by racy speech, rapid thoughts, and a plethora of ideas. These presentations have been useful and have resulted in significant breakthroughs in some of her assignments. The negative aspect of the illness was shown when she stopped taking her medication in the Abu Nazir plot line, and all the negative aspects of mania were also depicted, including symptoms such as: a lack of risk inhibition, the elusiveness of sleep, sexual disinhibition, isolation from friends and family, and drinking. It is good to see the media being used positively to educate viewers on mental illness. The *Homeland* series has been praised by several mental health organisations and advocates. The National Alliance on Mental Illness notes that the series portrays mental illness with "compassion, clarity and responsibility".

There have also been good plays, such as *Melancholia*, a play written by Lars von Trier. It shows the internal struggles of a person with depression in a powerful way. The central character, Justine, sabotages her own wedding and is in a near-catatonic state for most of the play.

There is a lot more that needs to be done by journalists, scriptwriters, producers, paparazzi, editors, and the owners of social media platforms.

The caveat for now is that the community should take information on mental illness from the media with a pinch of salt.

There is the sometimes erroneous posit that films are meant to entertain the public and not educate them. Ryan Howes PHD has argued that: *"What we see on TV or in the movies is therefore several times more dramatic, dangerous, condensed, frightening and/or bizarre than reality," he said. A screenwriter's job, he noted, is to create larger-than-life stories that capture viewers, are artistic representations and drive ticket sales. "It's not up to them to provide us with a balanced and nuanced education." (On the other hand, it is the news media's job to provide accurate information.)*

The opinions highlighted above drive the media, especially film scriptwriters and producers. As much as we would like to be entertained, there is a responsibility that we should all carry to ensure we convey and educate the right information do not misinform.

An accurate portrayal helps to break the barriers and at the same time educates. I recognise the fact that mental illness presents differently in different people and no two people are alike. Mental health exists on a multiple spectrum where many different factors intersect to paint a unique picture of each situation and everyone.

One of the best ways to do that is to replace negative stories that depict the symptoms surrounding mental illness with positive stories of the same individuals and their bravery in the face of their demons. By highlighting courage under fire, so to speak, and successful recoveries, the media can do more to revise misconceptions about neurological conditions than anything else can.

This will go a long way towards educating the masses, that such individuals should be understood from a perspective that may be different from the one they are used to. The result will be an increase in employment opportunities, affordable housing and educational opportunities. All 3 elements can go a long way towards alleviating chronic poverty and reducing homelessness among the neurologically ill.

In other words, if the media depicts the mentally ill in a positive light, it can teach people that they should not be treated differently. After all, can you feel good about yourself if you are constantly told that you are different from others, flawed and a threat to your loved ones? We need a society that not only rejects such premises, but also strives to create support services and groups that can alleviate misunderstandings.

Unfortunately, people are generally largely ignorant when it comes to understanding mental illness. The average individual may not even know the symptoms, treatments, and conditions of common ailments, such as depression and anxiety. This gap in education leads to fear, which leads to misunderstandings. Many believe that those with mental illness should just 'pull themselves together', not realising that they have to work way harder than they do to act and feel normal.

In a world where there is such a high level of stigma about mental illness, it would be great to see the media change the narratives in the same way that both *Homeland* and *Melancholia* have done so successfully.

Chapter 5

CULTURAL ATTITUDES REGARDING MENTAL ILLNESS IN THE BAME COMMUNITIES

Black Asian and Minority Ethnic (BAME) people have the short end of the stick when it comes to mental health care in the UK. Despite government efforts and the introduction of policies, these individuals are marginalised when it comes to their physical health already.

Ethnic issues have been a point of contention in the United Kingdom. It is a known fact that a discrepancy exists between mental health policies and how they are implemented. There have been several researches and accounts of the dis-crimination in the treatments received by the different ethnic groups. What is sad to see is that those in the BAME community are diagnosed with mental health issues more than their 'whiter' counterparts.

Risk Factors for BAME Communities' Mental Health

The Black Asian and Minority Ethnic community in England make up to one-fifth of the population. There are several factors that could account for the high number of people in the BAME community being diagnosed with mental health issues. There appear to be several reasons that may be the causative factor. People from the BAME community often face individual and societal challenges that can affect their access to healthcare and overall mental and physical health.

Social and educational Inequalities - Unemployment rates are higher among the BAME compared to their white counterparts. They are paid less even when they have similar qualifications and experience.

Racism and discrimination - People from BAME communities experience racism in their personal lives. We know that experiencing racism can be very stressful and has a negative effect on someone's overall health and mental health. Furthermore, there is a growing body of research that suggests those exposed to racism may be more likely to experience mental health problems, such as psychosis and depression.

Mental health stigma - In most BAME communities, mental illness and issues are taboo topics rarely spoken about and can be seen in a negative light. This attitude creates a massive barrier that stops people within the community from speaking out if they have a mental health problem or from seeking help. This stigma also discourages engagement with health services. Different communities understand and talk about mental health in different ways.

Criminal justice system - The David Lammy Independent Review looked into the treatment of, and outcomes for, BAME individuals in the Criminal Justice System. It identified there was growing concern over the unmet mental health needs of BAME individuals within the criminal justice system, particularly in the youth justice system. The *Review of the Youth Justice System in England and Wales*, prepared in 2016, found that over 40% of children in the Criminal Justice System are from BAME backgrounds, and more than one-third have a diagnosed mental health problem. The report further highlighted that the needs of BAME young people may be even greater than this, as it is likely they will have undiagnosed mental health problems or learning disabilities when they enter the justice system.

Migration

Housing and so many other factors

Of course, it is a known fact that people from the BAME communities experience racism in various areas of their lives, which ranges from attacks in their personal lives and a lack of job opportunities to verbal and physical abuse, poor housing and low educational attainment. The consequent effect of such racist treatment can cause stress that has a long-term effect on their mental health. In addition, there is a growing body of research that suggests people exposed to racism may be more likely to experience mental health problems, such as psychosis and depression.

This is understandable if we consider the fact that BAME communities face more barriers when it comes to receiving relevant and culturally appropriate aid. This includes a serious lack of cultural understanding, communication, and accessibility issues regarding appropriate health centres. Most also face barriers when so-called 'specialists' fail to understand the social and familial issues that are inherent to their indigenous culture and lifestyles.

To prevent this gap from getting bigger, service providers should be trained to work closely with people from BAME communities before they are allowed to diagnose them. An understanding of their cultural backgrounds, religious affinities, family and social life could go a long way towards improving their understanding of this community. Reviews may also help BAME community members to get the help they need via appropriate changes.

Unfortunately, psychiatry in the United Kingdom follows a strictly Eurocentric pattern, which has a negative effect on how BAME communities are treated and diagnosed. To make the improvements that are required, service providers that work with BAME community members should become more culturally competent. This includes in-depth analysis of not only people's different cultures but also the influence they have on their thinking.

Cultural differences play a huge role in how people seek any healthcare service. The biases and stigma associated with mental health issues aside, how different communities perceive their mentally sick members has a great deal of influence on this as well. Due to this, service providers have to combat not only general bias, but also the unconscious way that such communities treat mentally sick individuals.

That is because mental illness is a conversation that is taboo in several BAME communities. In addition, there is a declining socioeconomic structure and inequality, which means mental health is not usually given as much priority as it should be. Socio-economic uncertainties, coupled with taboos, have led to a decline in early interventions that could otherwise nip several neurological issues in the bud. This also leads to a reluctance of using mental health services, until it reaches the point where it becomes a crisis.

In some communities, mental health issues are deeply personal and seeking professional help is usually considered to be shameful and a disgrace; therefore, it's become a big elephant in the room. Added to that, many BAME communities do not speak English or do not know the language at all in the UK, so you have a community that is largely ignored.

This leads to individuals who do not have the language or confidence to tell service providers about their experiences, two facts that are crucial for them to understand what they are working with. The satisfaction rate for individuals with mental health issues and service providers who can speak English fluently in the UK is higher compared to the non-English speaking community.

That is not to say that every BAME community faces similar issues. Different ethnic groups have different experiences, as well as cultural and socioeconomic issues that result in mental health problems that are particular to them. For example, the black community based in the UK is more likely to:

• Experience an adverse effect from treatments.
• Be diagnosed with mental health issues.

- Be admitted into a hospital for their mental health concerns.
- Be disconnected from services, thus making their mental health worse.

There are a few reasons for these factors but the ones that stand out are: difficulty in integrating, racism and poverty. If you add to that the failure of most mental health service providers to understand or offer services that are culturally acceptable to such communities then it is clear you have several communities on the verge of collapse. Services that are accessible to white people in the UK are unacceptable to their non-white and non-English speaking counterparts for reasons that we discussed before. In fact, the former is usually 'over-diagnosed' when BAME community members seek services.

Due to the 'over-diagnosis' or 'misdiagnosis' of BAME, especially the black ethnic minority, several families would rather not report incidents of mental illness to the clinical setting because they fear being given an acute mental health diagnosis. Invariably, almost 65% of people with mental illness in the community have undiagnosed mental health issues and are thereby not receiving necessary treatment.

To understand the scale of the discrepancy and discrimination, perhaps an overview is needed of BAME communities and how they are treated by mental and physical health care service members. Doing so could help us to understand not only what these professionals have to work with, but also the barriers they face in understanding such communities.

Irish People

In March 2004, a conference was held that looked at the worrying health experiences of both the Irish and Irish Traveller communities in the UK. It focused on the lack of awareness of this problem and the resource allocation that is needed to address these health inequalities.

The conference looked at the 'Health inequalities and the Irish Community – Challenging Irish Invisibility'. It is known that Irish people who live and work in the UK have a higher rate of hospital visits and admissions than other BAME groups and there is a reason for this. Tragically, the Irish people have some of the highest rates of depression and drinking problems, which leads to strong suicidal tendencies.

The high rates of suicide and depression may stem from the social disadvantages they face in the United Kingdom. Besides a poor housing system, they face social isolation, which whittles away at their psychological state more than anything else. Add to this the fact that there is insufficient funding for BAME communities, and we have a situation where people are facing an uphill battle while they search for relevant services. Sarah Curtis in her book, *Health and Inequality: Geographical Perspectives*, demonstrates that there is a clear geographical disparity in the risk of developing mental illness, and the contextual and individual aspects of cultural life may be important in accounting for this variation in mental health. Given that mental health varies considerably between societies and cultures, geographical inequality exists in the perceived mental health of people living in culturally separate communities.

A research report commissioned by Irish Community Care Merseyside in 2005 stated that the "Wirral Irish community appears to experience disproportionate psychological distress, a first generation problem that has not dissipated, extending to subsequent generations. Initial struggles of adjustment and integration, stressful working and poor living conditions were contributing factors for the onset of mental ill-health amongst the Irish migrants. Exacerbated by the nervous tension from the problems brought in the wake of 'The Troubles', social exclusion and the collective shame attached to mental health, the situation has far from improved."

Most Irish immigrants come to the UK to find better work opportunities that can help them support their families or start life anew. Many came as teenagers (mainly between 15 and 18 years of age) and try to survive in a country rife with racism. Even though they speak English, it does little to alleviate their discomfort or allow them to make enough to make ends meet.

Even though Irish people are 'white', the challenges they face are like those that other ethnic minorities have faced.

Bronwen Walter in '*Mapping Irish Health*' shows the inadequacies, from a health perspective, of the ethnic category for the White Irish in the 2001 census. Walter states that the 2001 census fails in its intended purpose of including those people with an 'Irish cultural background'. It remains unclear as to whether it represents Irish descendants (second and third generation Irish). From this, Walter implies an obvious need to disaggregate the 'White' category. The census also shows that the self-reported health of the 'White Irish' is much closer to the pattern of other minority ethnic groups instead of the 'White British'.

The link between racial minorities and poor mental health has been established. Separate research suggests that the cumulative effects of mental health inequality generate intense concentrations of demand for mental health care in disadvantaged areas and this, in turn, leads to poor experiences and an inferior level of care provision. However, as most of the research has concentrated on black male ethnic minorities, the focus has been on the visible minorities and not the invisible minorities. It can be argued that if a community is not visible, its needs are not visible.

Fast-forward a couple of decades and they are too old to take care of themselves much less hold down a job. Degenerative diseases, such as diabetes and arthritis, make life difficult to bear and loneliness can eat away at them, especially if they do not marry. At that time, most of them are still living alone in a small room which has seen better days. They cannot go back home to Ireland because one, they cannot afford to and two, everyone they loved is dead, dying or has forgotten them.

Unfortunately, this is the story of most immigrants who came to the UK after World War II to find work. Besides the loneliness and deteriorating health, they also reported experiencing sexual and physical abuse through their stay. There are other stories as well that reveal the dark underbelly of British society, which include incidences of rampant racism.

African-Caribbean or the Black Community

When it comes to mental health issues in the UK, the black and Afro-Caribbean community cannot be ignored. They account for the highest number of service users of mental health services. In fact, this demographic is 5 times more likely to suffer from schizophrenia.

What is tragic is that most of these individuals do not get treatment willingly or seek it out for that matter. Most African-Caribbean people get mental health aid through 2 routes, the court, or the police. Many shy away from primary care, which is the usual treatment route for most people in the UK. Plus, this community is also more likely to be treated under the Mental Health Act and receive medication rather than diagnostic treatments such as psychotherapy.

The main reason for this is the fact that the black community remains wary of these services, and this exacerbates their condition. This is also because most of these services take a biased and coercive approach to convince them to seek treatment.

When we consider the fact that this community is constantly under attack, either by systemic or via personal racist tendencies, this is understandable. The Angry Black Woman stereotype is based on a reality in which women are expected to be perfect, but that reality does not hold in a community that has to fight discrimination at every turn.

To understand the cognitive processes of the African community, we have to understand some of the back story that has made this community what it is today. The general narrative that they base their beliefs on goes something like this: "We made it to this land in the hold of ships and survived slavery. This means we can survive whatever life throws our way." When this attitude does not work, they turn to prayer. While having a religious mindset is not a bad thing, when it is used to ignore serious health issues, it can result in irreversible consequences.

African-Caribbean who want to discuss the impact of racism on mental health face barriers that are not of their own making. Many are unable to find mental health practitioners who are not only skilled, but who are also culturally competent enough to help them heal. Large inequalities in care are apparent, not only in the lack of appropriate mental health advocates but also in the overuse of medications. This is due to misunderstandings regarding cultural expressions of mental distress.

Unfortunately, it is not easy to locate mental health practitioners who are proficient in anti-racist practices and strategies that are not oppressive. The issue is especially prominent outside most urban areas.

The issue could be resolved if more black individuals were trained to become mental health practitioners. Equipped with the same cultural background, tendencies, and upbringing, these professionals have more chances of getting through to the African community than their white counterparts.

To that end, there should be more recruitment and training of mental healthcare practitioners of African descent. However, current practitioners should also be trained in methodologies that are culturally and ethnically appropriate.

It is important to note that even a black mental healthcare provider can show racist tendencies. To understand this better, let us take the example of a black woman who describes her aches and pains when trying to talk about her depression. A medical practitioner who does not understand her issues on a personal level will probably relate her condition to a physical ailment rather than a mental one. Similarly, a black man who is suffering from a mood disorder or PTSD is likely to be told that he has schizophrenia.

Even black women who are more educated than Caucasian women can lag behind when it comes to getting appropriate mental health care. That is one of the reasons why the rate of people with depression is 50% higher in the former than in the latter. The fact that black men are treated similarly means that, in general, the community accounts for 45% of mental health needs in the country.

Cost is also a large factor when it comes to this community gaining access to appropriate mental healthcare facilities. That is because this demographic, like most individuals in the BME community, does not have access to health insurance. However, this could be rectified if mental health assessments were included in primary care, which, in turn, would reduce the need for expensive specialised care significantly. If these methodologies were used in time, they could make early interventions much more effective than they currently are. By interventions, we mean appropriate medication and lifestyle changes that could prevent the need for costly mental healthcare.

There is also a need for activism and monitoring of mental healthcare that could ultimately expand health insurance coverage and make affordable mental health care a reality. One solution is the introduction of support groups that are based in the community and focus on faith-based practices as much as therapeutic practices. This would go a long way towards resolving acceptability issues.

Similarly, courses such as first aid for mental health for professionals would assist such communities and make early detection possible. Referrals that can point to appropriate services can also reduce the lifelong and negative impacts of serious ailments. In other words, mental healthcare could be made accessible for the black community if coordinated efforts were made across the healthcare system. This includes activism and advocacy that can give rise to sustainable policies, which can trigger conversations across workplaces and places of worship.

Currently, much could be done to prevent the mental health of this community getting worse. Individuals in the community are at an increased risk of developing a neurological ailment if they are homeless or exposed to violence at an early age. Both these issues increase the risk of serious mental ailments such as depression and PTSD. However, the good news is that these conditions could be nipped in the bud with the introduction of inclusive health reforms and by training mental health practitioners in inclusive methodologies.

Historically speaking, faith, community, and spiritual beliefs tend to be influential sources of strength and support in the black community. When it comes to receiving emotional support, many members of the African community rely on their families and communities instead of professional mental healthcare experts. Their reliance on their communities is strong, even if they need proper therapeutic treatment.

While faith in the Divine can aid the recovery process to a certain extent, it should not be the only option the African community members have at their disposal. Plus, many of these spiritual communities are known for stigmatising professional healthcare in favour of divine intervention, which makes things even worse.

This can be avoided if these people are educated about mental disorders and the treatment processes that can help them manage these conditions or even cure them. This can be done if medical practitioners use the community to their advantage since that is mostly where the community members get most of their care from. For example, public education campaigns, open information sessions at local clinics, and educational presentations at community venues, such as Black churches, can ensure a wide swathe of this population is made aware of the solutions at hand.

Individuals who are comfortable with conventional treatments have a unique opportunity to make a difference that could herald new pathways that make mental healthcare accessible. However, the process could also be demystified by the practitioners if they encouraged patients to see care treatments right through to the end.

This can be done if the expected outcomes, number of sessions, and ultimate goals of the treatment are clearly outlined in advance. That way, the community could overcome the belief that the practices are coercive and, at the same time, remain in control of their own treatment.

In other words, the advantage that psychotherapy offers to the mind and recovery should be explained to made more obvious and less intimidating for the African community members. This would ensure they got the help they need, when they need it, and not when their condition has got as bad as it can be. That may be easier said than done for people who often take on multiple jobs to make ends meet, but it is still a possibility. The trick is to make these individuals understand that their mental health deserves the same priority as their ability to earn income for their families.

The Asian Community

The stats regarding the number of Asians in the UK who suffer from mental health issues are inconsistent. However, what this implies is that this ethnic minority community may have members of the community who are suffering mental health issues and have not had access to the mental health services for support. One of the key issues for us to remember is that the barrier to mental health is the story of most migrant communities. They are susceptible to psychological distress that may be the result of pre and post migration trauma and also the peer pressure to acclimatise in a society that is foreign to their own, as well as other issues that reduce their quality of life significantly.

While there are higher rates of recovery from schizophrenia, suicide rates among young and older Asian women are on the rise. While the former is attributed to strong family groups, the latter stems from adherence to cultural beliefs and values – the same formula that we have seen in the ethnic groups.

Similarly, most mental health issues in this group are also linked to Western approaches to treatment which are inappropriate to the needs of the Asian community. This is understandable because, unlike modern mental health practices, which focus on one ailment at a time, Asian people perceive individuals as an accumulation of body, mind, and spirit. For them, a person is a spiritual, emotional, and physical being who has everything he/she needs for self-healing.

This has its roots in the fact that the South Asian population has a bigger notion of 'shame' than other communities that reside in the UK. Many Asians fear that admitting they have a mental illness to their families will result in censure from their own community. With priority given to marriage and the need to shove 'shameful thoughts' and tendencies under the rug, the rise of mental health issues in the Asian community in the UK is a powder keg just waiting to blow.

Most disregard mental issues and put them down to superstitious beliefs. Besides this, language barriers also prevent this community from coming forward, which has more to do with vocabulary than anything else. For instance, there is no word for the term 'depression' in the many languages this community speaks. Identified causes are usually attributed to personal upheavals rather than specific neurological disorders.

One of the barriers is the fact that many in the community will not even think of going to their doctor if they are low in mood or have low level mental health issues. Of course, what this means is that the chances of being referred to see a therapist will be slim. The perception is that symptoms of depression they may be experiencing are personal issues that they can deal with.

Discussing mental health issues are not common conversation in this community. The lack of discussion about mental issues and the fact that talking about them will pose a risk to a family's reputation and status in the community prevents several Asians from seeking the right treatment. Many Asians attribute mental illnesses to either black magic, the will of God, or bad parenting. While bad parenting does lead to several mental ailments, the Asian community turns a blind eye to the other equally harmful causes. This includes child sexual harassment, which is a growing concern in this group due to the community's insistence on living in large and close-knit family units.

Chapter 6

THE ROLE OF THE GOVERNMENT

The government certainly plays a major role in influencing the direction of the way that communities view mental health and well-being, from Central Local Government to Local Authorities, Council Services, Social Care, Schools, Housing, Parks, and hospitals. The list is endless. Their role should include ensuring that the fabric of mental health support and well-being is strong enough to absorb those who may be in crises and to make sure services are put in place to encourage early intervention.

According to Councillor Izzi Seccombe OBE, Chairman of the LGA Community Wellbeing Board, the role of the government is to "*change perceptions of mental health, so that people think of their mental health as akin to their physical health. It is something that we have to look after; we can make ourselves stronger, but sometimes people are unwell. We can all help to make sure they are treated, supported, recover, and get back on their feet – exactly the same as when someone is physically unwell."*

We need to move away from just focusing on mental ill-health to helping everyone stay mentally well, providing community support and helping people to continue with their lives. Fundamentally, good mental health is good for our society and our economy.

In the UK, the National Health Service (NHS) has introduced several policies and taken initiatives that aim to reduce the obstacles to mental health care and services for ethnic and minority communities in the UK.

However, while the disparities between these groups and the nation's white population have been debated and researched extensively, there is little evidence to suggest that there has been any significant progress for black and minority ethnic groups. In fact, mental health services for the BAME communities have not seen any significant change.

At present, there is no national policy or strategy specifically put in place for the ethnic minority community to improve the BAME communities' access to mental health other than those that are already in place. Experiments to introduce treatments that are ethnically sensitive have been fragmented or selective. Due to this, the BAME groups continue to be marginalised or ignored completely. Even the Mental Health National Framework (MHNSF) and the NHS's plan for mental health do not take the mental health needs of BME communities into account. There have been calls from various Voluntary Sector Organisations requesting a more ethnocentric approach to care and treatment of people from this background.

The reforms that have been proposed fail before they have had a chance to work and there are two reasons for this. One, the suggested reforms have rarely been implemented and two, research based on organisational changes and service evaluations has largely ignored the ethnic and cultural aspects of service delivery.

This is concerning because, as per the **Under the Race Relations Amendment Act of 2000,** every organisation, including medical services, must have policies in place that take cultural diversity and ethnic equality into consideration when they are dispensing service. Every organisation must plan and deliver services and train staff in accordance with racial and ethnic requirements.

While there has not been significant progress in this regard, much can be done if certain regulations are put into practice. This includes:

Accountability and Ownership

One of the main reasons why general mental health practices have been unable to adapt to BAME communities is the severe lack of involvement from local communities. This is one of the main issues in many centrally managed services, such as the NHS, that have little to no system in place that can ensure local accountability.

This issue could be solved if clear lines of accountability and service ownership were encouraged via an inclusive and participatory approach to ethnic mental health services. By establishing local consultations and discussions between different agencies and key stakeholders, the situation could change for the better.

For instance, local mental health implementation teams should be encouraged to create formal methodologies that can encourage consumer involvement from minority and ethnic groups, including complementing primary care arrangements that can also encourage community and patient involvement in other services. Plus, these methodologies and arrangements should also be allowed to participate in service planning, delivery, effectiveness, and the evaluation of mental health services for BAME communities.

In other words, to improve mental health services and their implementation in BAME communities, local inclusivity and participation should be prioritised. This inside-out approach is not only the best way to ensure that locals are represented in the commission process; it will also ensure that quality standards and KPIs are met. In addition, to ensure locals have a say in such practices indefinitely, community representatives must be encouraged to follow clear and democratic processes.

This can be done with consistent clinical governance that provides a framework that can hold organisations such as the NHS accountable for maintaining the same high standards of care for the BAME communities as are enjoyed by the UK's white community. The good news is that those structures are already in place in mental health services, but they will need to be altered to suit minority and ethnic groups.

In addition, there should be a methodology in place that allows consumer feedback, especially for service users and their families. With consistent feedback from the local community as well as stakeholders, current mental health service models can be altered or replaced with relevant ones for certain groups. This method may be fragmentary, owing to the sheer number of ethnic groups in the nation, but with common methodologies and independent assessors, the approach can work wonders.

Therefore ethnicity should be prioritised when it comes to the clinical governance of the nation's mental health institutions, so that these groups have an appropriate platform to air grievances and give feedback for indigenous methodologies. Since BAME communities rely on families for emotional support, provisions should also be made for their loved ones.

With regular feedback from the locals and stakeholders, a common methodology complete with independent assessors is a possibility. Mental health organisations should also be responsible for evaluating staff regarding linguistic and cultural competencies. A thorough assessment of yearly reports on their progress can go a long way towards ensuring that ethnic and minority groups are given the same quality of care the white population currently enjoys.

One of the main requirements of service users in BAME communities, or of any service user in general, is the extent to which their requirements are evaluated and understood and what interventions are offered. To be effective, there should not be any discrepancies as per the ethnic and cultural backgrounds of these individuals.

However, this is far from the case today. There are several differences in the quality of mental health care, and these can be tracked if the focus is directed towards making organisations more capable of handling cultural inequalities, irrespective of the background of the patients using their services.

This is more than just about making mental health services culturally sensitive – it is about increasing awareness of those needs and improving the quality of care via equal services for all those who seek mental health aid. Besides dealing with cultural issues appropriately, this will also improve the overall support, care, evaluation, and treatment that is provided to BAME communities.

Chapter 7
COMMON MENTAL HEALTH ISSUES

A ccording to the National Institute for Health and Care Excellence (NICE), the following conditions are some of the most common mental health concerns that most people (white/ethnic and minorities) suffer from:

Depression

People describe depression in different ways. It is not just feeling sad, having a bad day or 'feeling blue'. Contrary to popular belief, depression is not a single mental ailment. It is sometimes a combination of several other forms of conditions. Some of the common symptoms include:
- Persistent low moods
- A loss of interest and pleasure in activities
- Changes in appetite; eating too much or eating less
- Trouble sleeping despite fatigue or sleeping too much

- Feelings of worthlessness and guilt
- Suicidal and other harmful thoughts
- Loss of confidence and poor self-esteem
- Loss of concentration, confusion and difficulty making decisions
- A feeling of pessimism
- Suicidal feelings
-

The symptoms above are by no means exhaustive. Please note that the symptoms of depression differ from person to person. These symptoms can reduce the quality of life of any individual who suffers from depression. The death of a loved one, the end of a relationship, relocation stress, and other experiences can cause emotional upheavals and sadness, but if those emotions persist, they are indicative of mental illness.

The grieving process is natural and while it may share some similarities to depression, it is far from being so. These two emotional tendencies differ from one another in the following ways:

Grief comes in waves since it is often triggered by memories of the deceased or lost loved ones. Depression, on the other hand, can result in an absence of these emotions which prevents the individuals from processing their experience, leading to harmful tendencies.

Grief usually does not lead to a loss of self-esteem. Depression, on the other hand, can lead to feelings of worthlessness and self-loathing. In other words, depression makes individuals turn inwards and most of them do not reach out to others for support. Since grief-stricken people do not close themselves off completely, they attract the support they need naturally. This is one of the main reasons why clinically depressed people start hating themselves and start to believe that they are unloved.

Depression does not discriminate. Even a person who looks fine on the outside and lives a normal life may be going through a depressive episode inside. This can be due to several reasons:

- Differences in certain chemicals in the brain, which then leads to symptoms of depression.
- Genetics – contrary to popular belief, depression is not just an effect of traumatic circumstances, it can also be inherited genetically. For instance, if a

twin has depression, the other twin may suffer from the same later in life.

- People who have low self-esteem or are under a lot of stress may consistently have pessimistic thoughts that may be a sign of depression.
- Individuals who are neglected, abused, or exposed to violence may suffer from chronic depression.
- Alcohol or drug abuse.
- Serious or chronic illnesses, such as cancer, insomnia, or heart disease.

Types of Depression

The Diagnostic and Management Guidelines for Mental Disorders in Primary Care, ICD-10, give guidelines on how to determine if the depression is mild, moderate, or severe. The causes and effects of depression do not imply that the word is an umbrella term for the condition. Since there is no one cause of the disorder, there is not only one type of depression. It can take a few different forms. Some of the more common types of depression include:

Dysthymia – Also known as Persistent

Depressive Disorder, Dysthymia can lead to low moods that last for up to two years. Individuals who are diagnosed with this depressive disorder may suffer from severe or mild symptoms throughout the duration of their ailment.

Postpartum depression – Also known as the 'baby blues', this affects some women right after they give birth. Depending on the severity of the condition, they can suffer from mild anxiety or low moods that last for two weeks. Some women can also suffer from full-blown depression during their pregnancy or after suffering from the symptoms of postpartum depression. Persistent feelings of sadness and anxiety, coupled with the exhaustion of giving birth, can make their condition chronic, which can prevent the mothers from taking care of their babies.

Psychotic depression – This is triggered by certain types of psychosis, which can be anything from disturbing beliefs, delusions, or persistent hallucinations. It is often linked with depressing themes, such as poverty, illness, and guilt – the three main factors that contribute to depression in BME communities.

115

Seasonal affective disorder – This type of depression usually sets in during the winter when natural sunlight is scarce and then lifts during the warmer months. This can be accompanied by social withdrawal, more sleep, as well as weight gain.

Bipolar disorder – Individuals who suffer from bipolar disorder can experience episodes of extreme sadness or extreme joy (hypomania) without warning.

Anxiety Disorder

Anxiety is a common emotional and natural reaction to trauma or danger. We all experience anxieties at different times in our lives. Anxiety can vary in its expression, from mild to severe. The duration can vary too, from a few minutes to years.

Anxiety is termed as a disorder when it:
• Interferes with the person's ability to work or their relationships
• It is severe and the effect is long

Generalised Anxiety Disorder (GAD)
This anxiety is characterised by a constant and

116

general feeling of worry that is overwhelming. The worry is persistent, and it is usually about what could go wrong, with their health, work, and sometimes even basic things such as the door being jammed, immigration, the economy, family, and financial issues. They are prone to focus on a few problems at a time. Being late for an appointment can become a big issue because they believe something bad will happen to them if they do not follow set patterns.

The signs and symptoms of GAD can last up to six months or just a day, depending on the severity of the trauma or ailment. Individuals with GAD may also suffer from other related disorders, such as depression and social phobia. Sadly, many persons diagnosed with GAD resort to drugs and alcohol to numb these symptoms, which leads to a series of physical ailments, such as migraines, persistent fatigue, irritability, hard muscle tension, concentration issues, insomnia, and bowel issues.

GAD may also be triggered by a combination of factors which include:

Biological factors – Changes in brain chemicals that can lead to GAD.

Genetics – Most people who suffer from GAD also have a history of the mental disorder in their families. However, this does not mean that a person will develop anxiety if a close family member suffers from this condition as well.

Traumatic events – For BME communities, stressful events that can cause GAD include difficulty acclimatising to foreign communities. In general, individuals who lose a close relative, job, or house, or those who get separated from their parents and experience other traumatic events can develop GAD.

Psychological issues – Certain personality traits can lead to GAD as well. For example, individuals who are oversensitive, emotional, perfectionists, or intolerant to stimuli may suffer from this mental health issue.

Since the anxiety that generates from GAD cannot be controlled, the condition is often hidden by those who suffer from it. Many people do not understand what they are going through and put it down to their lack of self-worth. This demoralisation is a common cause, with many sufferers becoming discouraged, unhappy, and ashamed of carrying out normal routines. Therefore GAD is often linked with depression, which makes accurate diagnosis challenging.

Panic Disorder

Contrary to popular belief, a panic attack is different from a panic disorder. If an individual feels tired and overstressed due to excessive exertion, they may suffer from shortness of breath, which is indicative of a panic attack. This tendency is triggered by an effect. A panic disorder, on the other hand, is unpredictable and unexpected.

This disorder is common in people who also suffer from GAD since the feeling is similarly persistent. This mental health ailment is characterised by persistent symptoms of fear which can include chest pain, shortness of breath, dizziness, and heart palpitations. Since these symptoms are also indicative of heart disease, the condition is often misdiagnosed.

Oftentimes, an accurate diagnosis comes after extensive and costly medical procedures fail to provide a correct diagnosis, which, in turn, aggravates the condition. It is not uncommon to see patients develop anxiety during their treatment, especially those who also have to overcome language barriers.

Panic disorders are often triggered if the individual feels as if he/she is about to die. It can also arise due to certain situations which may not seem as serious to anyone who does not suffer from the condition.

Most people who suffer from panic disorders avoid stressful situations to prevent the symptoms from manifesting. Situational triggers can be external or internal depending on the severity of the condition and the lifestyle of the individual. Anxiety can lead to pervasive avoidance of certain situations, such as being home alone, travelling by car or bus, being on a lift or bridge, or being in a crowded space. While these situations may seem harmless, they take on fearful proportions for people who suffer from this ailment.

Obsessive-Compulsive Disorder

Obsessive-compulsive disorder (OCD) is a persistent and chronic mental health disorder which causes uncontrollable and recurring thoughts and behavioural patterns. These obsessions and compulsions trigger repetitive ticks, behaviours, and tendencies that prevent the victim from leading a normal life.

People with OCD may suffer from obsessions, compulsions, or both at the same time. To understand what victims go through, we need to understand what these two terms mean.

Obsessions refer to repetitive urges or mental images that trigger anxiety. This can be anything from hypochondria (an abnormal anxiety about your health), aggressive thoughts towards themselves or others around them, or a tendency to ensure everything they own is set up symmetrically.

Compulsions, on the other hand, refer to repetitive behaviour patterns that an individual suffering from OCD may feel the urge to do in response to the obsessive thoughts. We can say that

OCD-based compulsions are caused by those unnatural obsessions. This can include compulsive counting, cleaning (self or surroundings), repeatedly checking on certain things (such as ensuring that the doors are locked or the oven is off, among others).

While not all rituals or habits are compulsive, individuals who suffer from OCD take them to new heights. That is because they are unable to control their thoughts even though they realise that those thoughts are excessive. In fact, most OCD patients spend an hour a day on those thoughts and behaviours which can increase if they feel relieved afterwards.

Many people who suffer from OCD also develop motor tics, such as twitching eyes, excessive blinking, repetitive or brief uncontrollable movements, grimacing, shrugging, or jerking heads. Common tics can also include persistent throat clearing, grunting, and snorting.

Depending on the severity of the condition, these symptoms can either worsen with time or come and go erratically. Victims often try to avoid situations that can trigger their obsessions and compulsions, or they turn to substance abuse to numb themselves. Even though most of them realise that what they are doing is not normal, they are powerless to stop it. Some adults and children may not even realise that their behaviour is abnormal, which can lead to anxiety and social isolation.

Post-Traumatic Stress Disorder

Post-Traumatic Stress Disorder or PTSD is a mental health disorder that is triggered by certain traumatising events. As mentioned in a previous chapter, this can result from either witnessing or experiencing highly distressing events or incidents. Most victims who face traumatic events may find adjusting to a normal life challenging. This can be prevented with timely self-care, but if symptoms are allowed to get worse, they can last for years. They can start within a month of the traumatic event(s) and cause difficulties in social and work situations, as well as relationships. However, symptoms may also appear a year after experiencing the traumatic events. Either way, they can interfere with the victim's ability to function normally or hold a steady job for that matter.

There are four types of symptoms that PTSD victims suffer from, namely avoidance, intrusive memories, negative mood swings/persistent negative thought, and physical/emotional reactions to triggers. Depending on the traumatic event and severity of the condition, the symptoms can vary from one person to the next.

Some people who go through trauma and have PTSD may isolate themselves from their friends and family members or have difficulty communicating with them. This can lead to trust issues because of the way their loved ones react to their symptoms has a lot to do with how fast they recover.

Bipolar Disorder

Also known as manic depression, bipolar disorder is a mental health issue that leads to extreme mood swings, ranging from crippling depression to emotional highs or hypomania. There is no emotion in between, which means a person who is bipolar may feel completely hopeless one minute and euphoric the next. These mood swings prevent victims from thinking clearly and it can also lead to sleep, judgement, and behavioural issues.

Depending on the severity of the condition, mood swings can occur multiple times a day or rarely ever. Some people may experience symptoms in between swings, while others may seem completely normal. The condition usually lasts a lifetime, but it can be controlled with appropriate medication and psychological counselling.

While there is no single cause for this ailment, some factors can contribute to the manifestation of bipolar disorder, such as:

Genetics – Bipolar disorder can manifest in children whose parents or siblings have it as well. This is not set in stone though. Some children who have a family history of the disorder may never develop it. In fact, a twin may be bipolar while the other may be completely normal.

Stress – A traumatising or stressful event, such as the loss of a loved one, a serious injury, divorce or financial issues, can trigger a manic episode. If left uncontrolled, the negative thoughts that generate from the incident may lead to the development of the disorder.

Contrary to popular belief, there is no one cause for this condition. Depending on the severity of the traumatic incidents, stress, and the role genetics plays, people may suffer from one or more of the following types of bipolar disorders:

Bipolar I Disorder – Victims who suffer from this bipolar disorder have had at least one manic episode, followed, or preceded by severe depressive episodes. In certain cases, the manic episodes may also lead to psychosis.

Bi-Polar II Disorder – Victims who suffer from bipolar II disorder don't experience a manic episode, but they do experience depressive and hypomanic episodes.

It should be noted that bipolar disorder II is not a severe form of bipolar I disorder. It is a separate mental disorder and the difference lies in the duration of the symptoms. Even though individuals who suffer from bipolar I may suffer from severe and dangerous manic episodes, those who suffer from bipolar II may suffer for many more years in comparison.

Cyclothymic Disorder – Victims who suffer from cyclothymic disorder suffer from several hypomanic and depressive symptoms over a period of at least two years. This condition is often confused with depression.

Besides the symptoms above, there are certain symptoms of the condition can also be triggered by substance abuse or consumption of alcohol during a medical condition such as a stroke or multiple sclerosis. The disorder is usually diagnosed in their teens or early 20s.

Personality Disorder

Personality Disorder (PD) is a form of mental condition that affects how someone relates to others, their worldviews and perceptions. There are different types of PD.

Antisocial personality disorder

According to the NHS, this type of PD is a particularly challenging type that is characterised by impulsive, irresponsible, and often criminal behaviour. There is also a level of recklessness and disregard for other people's feelings. People with this diagnosis are typically manipulative and deceitful.

"A person with **antisocial personality disorder** may: exploit, manipulate or violate the rights of others, and lack concern, regret or remorse about other people's distress. They may also behave irresponsibly, show disregard for normal social behaviour, and have difficulty sustaining long-term relationships.

To understand antisocial personality disorder, we must look at the broader context, i.e. personality disorders. When a diagnosis of personality disorder is made, it refers to a persistent pattern of behaviour and experiences that derive from the victim's culture. The disorder can be inflexible and set in early adolescence before stabilising with time. If left unchecked, a personality disorder can lead to significant distress and mental impairment.

Individuals who suffer from anti-personality disorder persistently violate the rights of people around them. Most victims are diagnosed between the ages of 15 and 18, depending on the number of manic episodes they experience before reaching adolescence.

The symptoms differ according to their severity and individuals who exhibit dangerous or harmful behaviour patterns are usually deemed sociopathic and psychopathic. While these two tendencies share similarities, they are quite different from each other. Psychopaths can appear normal, even charming, but underneath they lack a conscience and empathy, making them manipulative and unpredictable and they often, but not always, have criminal tendencies. On the contrary, a sociopath typically has a conscience, but it is weak. They may know that what they are doing is wrong, and might feel some guilt or remorse, but that will not stop the behaviour. Both lack empathy; the ability to stand in someone else's shoes and understand how they feel. Both conditions share certain symptoms that can make them seem similar. This includes a complete disregard for laws, violation of the physical and emotional rights of others, a lack of remorse, consistently irresponsible behaviour, and a tendency to lie, among others.

While no exact cause is known for this mental disorder, certain genetic and environmental factors have been known to trigger symptoms. Victims who have family members with the same mental health issue are susceptible, especially if they have a parent with anti-social tendencies. There is a link, coupled with environmental factors, which means a sibling, or a child can develop such antisocial tendencies.

Chapter 8

THE ROLE OF DIET ON OUR MENTAL HEALTH AND MOOD

Do you know that there is a link between what we eat and how we feel?

When we sleep, our bodies go into a semi-vegetative state, but our brains do not sleep. The brain is responsible for our breathing, heart rate, and ensuring that blood flows to all the parts of our bodies where it is needed. It, therefore, needs a constant supply of fuel to remain active and keep us healthy. That fuel should come naturally from the food we eat, but the type of nutrition we consume has a lot to do with how well our brain carries out its functions.

Our nutritional intake has a direct effect on the structure and function of the brain which, in effect, means there is a link between what we eat and our mood. If we eat high-quality foods that contain

131

essential nutrients, such as vitamins, minerals, and antioxidants, our brains will be protected from oxidative stress. This is the waste or free radicals that the body produces when it uses oxygen. If left unchecked, that stress can damage cells which can lead to certain mental health issues.

Just like a car, the brain can be damaged if we consume anything less than premium fuel. Low-premium food or fuel refers to processed or refined food that is made of harmful substances that our brain cannot expel. For instance, food items that contain high levels of refined sugar can mess up our insulin production, trigger inflammation, and increase oxidative stress as a result. This is also linked to depression and other mood disorders, but the good news is that such mood disorders can be curbed with a healthy, brain-building diet.

Think about it, if the inflammatory free radicals are allowed free reign around the brain's enclosed space, then brain tissue damage will be imminent. Sadly, very few people are aware of the connection between nutrition and mental health even though they understand that there is a link between physical ailments and nutritional deficiencies. As mentioned before, this is the same disconnect that mental health service providers are guilty of today.

For example, depression is usually seen as a biochemical reaction that is based on emotion rather than lack of proper nutrition and irregular brain chemistry. On the contrary, diet and nutrition play a key role in the onset, severity, and development of this mental ailment. Many food patterns that precede the onset of depression occur during it as well, such as skipped meals, poor or complete loss of appetite, or a craving for sweet food. It is high time that mental health service providers realised there is a noticeably clear link between the nutrition our brain gets and human cognition and behaviour.

To understand this link better, let us revisit our discussion on prevalent mental health disorders in the UK – depression, OCD, and bipolar disorder in particular. Notably, the diet of patients who suffer from these mental health issues is severely deficient in essential minerals, vitamins, and omega-3 fatty acids.

These are usually treated with daily supplements of vital nutrients which can reduce the symptoms enough to make them manageable. For instance, supplements containing omega-3 fatty acids are known to reduce symptoms as they turn into neurotransmitters. These, in turn, reduce depression and other mental health disorders.

Therapeutic interventions, such as nutritional treatment, are used to control and prevent the onset of the mental health disorders, as well as ADD, ADHD, eating disorders, autism, and addiction. However, it should be noted that most prescription drugs also come with side effects that may aggravate an already exacerbated condition. This includes common antidepressants; whose side effects are so severe many patients prefer to skip them altogether.

Unfortunately, victims who skip these medications are usually on suicide watch or institutionalised for their own good. However, chronic, or higher doses of these drugs can lead to drug toxicity and even become life-threatening.

That is why alternatives such as nutritional therapy is considered along with the fact that intake can be adjusted, according to the results acquired through observation or changes in the patient.

What is undeniable is that the diet of someone going through depression or any other form of mental illness is far from healthy or adequate. Besides making poor food choices, they skip or overindulge on meals, which can make the condition worse. That is because a lack of proper nutrition leads to a reduction in serotonin levels – the chemical that our nerve cells produce which is supposed to regulate our mood. Is it any surprise that lower levels of this neurotransmitter are linked to higher suicide rates? If serotonin levels drop to a certain level, it can trigger impulsive and risky behaviour which can ultimately lead to this fatal conclusion.

There is an obvious link between diet and our mental health.

There is a need for us to check if our diet is making us anxious or depressed. We all may have woken up in a bad mood occasionally; it is common and not strange. I believe that if you often feel anxious or depressed and cannot seem to shake it, there's a chance your diet may have something to do with it.

Food and mood are intimately linked, and there are a few key culprits that may be having a significant effect on your mental state. A diet high in processed foods, sugar, aspartames, and chemicals has been shown to have a significant impact on mental health.

A 2013 study in Eating Behaviors Journal found a relationship between higher consumption of processed foods and anxiety, and another 2013 study in The International Journal of Yoga found that lower levels of refined and processed food consumption are linked to more positive attitudes.

Each individual suffering from these issues is unique and addressing food intake and digestive issues is just one aspect of the solution. That said, processed food, with its blend of sugar, unhealthy fats, and chemicals that cannot be found in nature, are often detrimental to those suffering from anxiety and depression.

Vitamin D

Studies have shown there is a link between depression and vitamin D deficiency. Vitamin D is known as the "sunshine" vitamin. It is an essential fat-soluble nutrient. It helps keep bones healthy and strong, helps cell growth, and benefits the immune function. The nutrient can be obtained through certain foods and dietary supplements, but our bodies absorb vitamin D primarily through sun exposure. If you do not get enough sunlight, you may develop vitamin D deficiency. People who have darker skin have greater amounts of melanin. Melanin reduces vitamin D production in the skin. The sun helps in the production of melanin and limited exposure to sunlight can lead to vitamin D deficiency.

Studies in 2016 confirmed that Vit D deficiency is more prevalent among Black Africans and Afro-Caribbean. Seasonal affective disorder is a form of depression that occurs mainly during the winter months and is thought to be linked to a lack of vitamin D caused by limited sun exposure.

The significance of nutrients for our mental health is undeniable. Here is a simple breakdown of certain nutritional essentials that need to be in our diet for optimum brain health.

Carbohydrates

Carbohydrates play a key role in brain health and development for a reason. These naturally occurring polysaccharides affect our behaviour and mood if consumed in appropriate quantities. They trigger the release of insulin, which directs our blood sugar into cells that need it for energy, and encourage the entry of tryptophan into the brain, which affects neurotransmitters.

People who eat food that is low in carbohydrates often fall into depression because their brains do not get adequate levels of tryptophan and serotonin that can prevent several symptoms from manifesting. This can be prevented by the consumption of food with a low Glycaemic Index (GI), such as fruit, vegetables, pasta, and grains. These nutritional choices are known to provide a lasting and moderate effect on brain chemistry as well as energy levels, compared to food that has high GI such as sweets.

Proteins

Proteins are composed of amino acids, which are pretty much the building blocks of bodies. Our body produces at least 12 of these, while the remaining 8 (essential amino acids) must be taken in externally via our diet. A diet that contains all the essential amino acids includes meat, eggs, dairy products, and milk. While you can take protein from a vegetarian diet (such as from peas, grains, and beans), it will be low in several essential amino acids.

The type of protein we consume affects how our brain functions and, consequently, our mental health as well. That is because most of the neurotransmitters we have in our brain are made up of amino acids. This includes dopamine (which is made of the amino acid tyrosine) as well as serotonin (which is made from tryptophan). If serotonin and dopamine levels drop in the body, it can disrupt the neurotransmitter synthesis in the brain which can lead to aggressive tendencies.

This can also lead to a build-up of amino acids to levels dangerous enough to cause permanent brain damage. For instance, an increase in phenylalanine in individuals who suffer from phenylketonuria (which causes intellectual disabilities, behavioural and seizures) can lead to massive brain damage.

Omega-3

To understand the role of omega-3 fatty acids or ω-3 fatty acids, we need to understand what the brain is comprised of. This organ is made up of many cell membranes which are made from a special type of fat, namely omega-3 fatty acid. All that grey matter is pure fat, but not the harmful kind.

We need healthy amounts of that fat to ensure that our central nervous system remains healthy and functions as it is supposed to. Essential fatty acids keep our neurones healthy and ensure that they fire impulses when needed. When this process stops working as it should, we can fall into a depressive state.

In fact, omega-3 or Dihydroxyacetone (DHA) is vital for brain development throughout our life. From our early cognitive development as babies to our learning abilities as adults, this essential fatty acid literally helps us think and feel.

Our brains are essentially 60% fat, out of which 20% is made up of these fatty acids. A pregnant woman who does not include this essential nutrient in her diet has more chance of giving birth to a child with a pre-existing mental health disorder than a woman who has sufficient omega-3 intake. That's because our brains work via a series of complex neurological networks. Signals from one brain cell or neurone travel to another, carrying messages that let our body know what it needs to do.

A single cell leaves another cell at the synapse and crosses a gap to the next neurone. However, for a smooth transition, these signals have to be capable or strong enough to penetrate the other's membrane, which is predominantly composed of fat. Ion channels in the membranes are responsible for allowing those signals to pass through in a continuous flow. It is DHA that makes these channels flexible enough to ensure that this flow is never interrupted.

This vital component is also responsible for synaptogenesis or the formation of synapses between the neurones. According to research, pre-natal babies who are given a diet that is deficient in omega-3 or DHA halve this procedure in the brain by about 50%.

When a woman is going through the last

trimester of her pregnancy, the brain of the unborn foetus develops by an impressive 260%. During this time, the mother has to have sufficient DHA intake during this critical time.

Once the baby is born, the brain continues to grow at a rapid pace. In fact, during the first year, it grows by a whopping 175%, which reduces to about 18% in year two. After the child passes 2 years of age, the total size of the brain increases in size by about 20% throughout childhood. The amount of omega-3 consumed is directly proportional to the volume of grey matter that develops so to speak.

Speaking of grey matter, people who have sufficient omega-3 in their diet are believed to have more of it than those who don't have enough, especially in the part of the brain that develops dopamine (aka the 'happy' hormone). This means people who have a DHA deficient diet are more likely to develop depression. This is also why some mothers suffer from post-natal depression – since most of the DHA in their body goes to the baby via breast milk, it leaves insufficient amounts in the mother, who cannot stave off depression.

Besides the DHA in omega-3, fish oil also contains essential fatty acids that reduce inflammation which can otherwise damage brain cells. Even though this inflammation can be the result of a natural result of injury, it can, if left untreated, lead to the development of neurological ailments, such as depression and insomnia.

So how do fatty acids keep depression at bay? To understand that we first need to understand how they work against each other. The thing is our brain needs a balance of omega-3 or ω-3 fatty acids, as well as ω-6 fatty acids, to function well. That equilibrium is important because these two acids compete to control said inflammation and thus, depression.

If, for instance, ω-3 fatty acids increase at the expense of the other, prostaglandin production is compromised. These are lipids that are made by a chemical reaction at the site where they are needed. Prostaglandins act as signals that trigger different processes in the body depending on where they are generated, including inflamed parts of the brain which, if left untreated, can lead to a high fever or worse.

There are several different types of this lipid in action at the site of inflammation. One, in particular, is responsible for ensuring that depression does not get out of control during a sickness. Think back to the last time you were so sick that you could barely get out of bed. Do you remember the feelings of loneliness and fear that you would never be able to recover? That behaviour is called sickness behaviour and it manifests due to the presence of a prostaglandin called E2. Many efficient anti-depressants are made to reduce PGE2 levels and other cytokines that can otherwise induce and maintain a depressive state.

Chapter 9

SOCIAL MEDIA, DEPRESSION AND SUICIDE

The average person spends approximately 2 hours per day on social media. That is about 5 years and 4 months spent worrying about what other people think of us and what we can post to make ourselves look happier than we really are.

This is unsurprising if we look at the facts. Social media applications, such as Facebook and Instagram, have more than a billion active users at any given time across the globe. Facebook alone has over a third of the world's population in its grip. That is a whopping number of people with multiple profiles who spend a lot of screen time scrolling through one type of content or another.

The main reason? Boredom – plain and simple. More than a third of the Earth's population is bored several times throughout the day and night and they are compelled to turn to screens that literally leech the life out of them. With more time spent perusing screens and little to no time spent with supportive peer groups, is it any wonder why depression and emotional disorders are rampant (and rising in number) among today's adolescents?

Countless studies have concluded that as social media gains in popularity, the number of mood disorders increases at the same time. But a question arises – does an excessive use of social media result in depression, or do depressed people tend to use it more, thus exacerbating their condition?

To answer this question, we need to understand how social online platforms hijack our minds. The bottom line is that every one of the platforms is designed to ensure that users remain online and active on their profiles for as long as humanly possible. That is the only way they can bombard us with enough advertisements to numb our judgement and trigger compulsive behaviour, such as unexplainable spending sprees.

To achieve this goal, social media applications are filled with triggers that reward us for staying online for as long as they need to convert us into paying customers for brands they are paid to endorse. In the same way that dopamine is released when we gamble or drink, social media is filled with triggers that release this hormone for as long as we are engaged. Simply put, if we want to get as many hits as we want, we spend as many hours it takes to get 'high' online.

By hits, we are, of course, referring to the likes, comments, and reactions to personal posts. The more hits we receive, the 'happier' we are so to speak. Since we take our social media profiles everywhere via mobile apps, we are constantly in a state of deprivation *and* exultation, a state of mind that ends that 'high' soon after it is generated.

That is how social media hacks our brains and makes us think that we are happier than we really are. Actual money is being spent on technologies and machinery that can stimulate this response in perpetuity so that we are constantly in buying mode.

When that stream of dopamine is cut off even for a few minutes, fear sets in. This is quickly accompanied by anxiety and crippling loneliness when we realise that reality is quite different from the impression which our online profile has given us. That is why it does not take a second for most of us to switch on our devices again for pleasure.

What is tragic is that most of us are powerless in the face of this tendency. Social media applications have algorithms working behind the scenes that are designed to both increase and maintain user engagement consistently. Users are made to engage with the same kind of content on a repetitive cycle without realising that they are being duped. This creates a bubble of sorts that the user fails to prick or see beyond.

Here is a simple example to help you understand this. Say a user clicks on a blog about a local event or comments on a post about certain events that have made their life miserable. Based on their comments, they will be bombarded with negative content in a bid to keep them engaged or to keep them stewing in their own juices so to speak. With emotional contagion added to the mix, perusing negative content has a seriously unhealthy effect on the individual's mental state.

We need to understand that social media addiction can trigger destructive tendencies, such as cyberbullying and a constant need for approval. This is understandable since most users tend to show the 'highlight reel' of their lives on social media and snip out content that they think is boring or will not get any reactions online.

When another user sees that reel, they compare it to their own life, which may not be as rosy as the one portrayed by their fellow user. This naturally leads to feelings of inadequacy, inferiority, and shame.

These feelings can trigger destructive approval-seeking tendencies under the anonymity that social media gives them. This includes cyberbullying, such as online harassment, that can induce similar destructive thoughts in their victims or trigger suicidal thoughts. Since they do not face their victims physically, cyberbullies are emboldened by the responses they get and the knowledge they are safe from the consequences of their actions.

Effects of Cyberbullying

Victims of cyberbullying engage in an increasing number of behaviours that allows them to forget their pain. In children, this can take on tragic proportions. Bullying in any shape or form can cause significant emotional distress to children and teenagers with developing minds. Here are just some harmful effects that they undergo:

Humiliation – Since cyberbullying takes place in cyberspace, it is well-nigh undetectable. The result is that children and teenagers are bullied and humiliated on online platforms that, in turn, exacerbate their state of mind with negative content.

Most cyberbullies pick their victims at random or from their circle of peers. Usually, they harass their target by posting embarrassing pictures of them online and spreading rumours that shame the latter. The bully usually threatens to expose the victim even if the victim has nothing to be fearful of. The sheer number of people who receive those embarrassing images and videos add to the intense feelings of humiliation that the victim feels which makes them believe they are social pariahs.

Feeling Overwhelmed and Vulnerable –
Cyberbullying can be crushing, especially if there is
more than one bully ganging up on the victim.
Because of this, victims can feel as if the entire world
is against them and that the situation is more than
they can handle. What makes the matter worse is
that they cannot even feel safe in their own homes
since cyberbullying does not have boundaries. It
invades homes through smartphones and PCs,
irrespective of the time of the day or night. In other
words, victims have nowhere to escape, which
exacerbates the fear they are already feeling.

Since the bullying occurs in cyberspace, it can
feel permanent. Today's kids know that once a piece
of information, such as an embarrassing picture, is
on the internet, it will be there forever even if they try
to have it taken down. That is just how Google's
algorithm works – even if the cache is removed, the
file can still remain in servers which a skilled hacker
can get into with some work.

Mostly, cyberbullies target the most vulnerable,
which is why they first target the person's worth and
value. Most people respond to those feelings with

harmful diversions, such as mutilation or cutting. For example, if a schoolgirl is bullied for being overweight and taunted online for it, she may force herself to adopt a crash diet or turn bulimic just so she can somehow make the bullying stop. Tragically, bullies are unrelenting, even if they see their victims making this effort. That is because they feel empowered when they bully individuals who are weaker than them. Since the internet provides anonymity, they have free rein to torture their victims as many times as they want and whenever they want.

In other words, the people they are bullying may not even know who is torturing them until it is too late to do anything about it. Kids may not even tell their parents about the bullying for fear that their computers and smart devices will be taken away, even if they know it is for their safety.

Anger and Suicidal Tendencies – Some victims turn angry and vengeful about what is happening to them, and they may take it out on others. If they decide to retaliate against the aggressors, the results can be devastating and fatal, especially with gun laws being as flexible as they are.

Many individuals lose interest in their own lives and relate to the world around them differently than others. All these feelings come together and lock them in a vicious cycle that they think they cannot get out of because their bullies are everywhere online. Unfortunately, the bullying does not stop offline. Cyberbullies often spread the same misinformation they use online in schools or social circles to complete the cycle and ensure the bullied are ostracised and isolated so that they remain their prime targets.

This can be particularly devastating for children who do not have friends and who are bullied online, as well as offline. While they could cut down on the negative stimuli by reducing the time they spent online, most of them don't since this measure would cut them off from the things they use to distract themselves, such as online games, social media, and even pornography.

This is also why children who are bullied online have a low attendance rate at their school compared to kids who are not bullied. Since the kids who torment them are relentless, they try and avoid them by skipping school as many times as they can. As a result, their grades take a nosedive, and even if they don't continue this absence from school, their constant feelings of anxiety and humiliation make schoolwork impossible, to say the least, which makes their emotional state even worse. In some cases, the victims either drop out of school completely or switch schools, and both scenarios can be devastating for their parents as well.

Victims of cyberbullying often fall into depression and suffer from other stress-related mental illnesses. After all, if your sense of worth is questioned and you are taken apart on a regular basis, wouldn't you feel as if the world is against you and that you do not deserve happiness?

In fact, the mental illnesses they suffer from can translate into physical ailments, such as stomach ulcers (which can result from an excess of stomach acid as the body goes into an alert state) and skin conditions. Some victims adopt bad eating habits, such as skipping entire meals, throwing up food right after they have eaten, or trying to drown their depression in food by binge eating. Some may also suffer from insomnia or nightmares that keep them up at night.

If these symptoms are ignored, or if the victim continues to suffer, they may lose all hope and try to take their own lives. This can happen if they believe that suicide is the only way they can escape the emotional and physical pain they are feeling. Tragically, this tendency is not apparent until it is too late to do anything to prevent it. Some victims may not even show the above-mentioned signs at all and, at first glance, may seem completely content and happy with their lives. However, they are the ones who need to be monitored more closely than those who show obvious signs of bullying since they are internalising their suffering and thus worsening their already frail mental health.

If your child or someone you know is being cyberbullied, telling them to keep a stiff upper lip will only make them feel more isolated and alone than they already are. The correct measure, and one that will not make them withdraw into themselves, is daily communication and steps that can end their torment. In other words, rather than encouraging them to ignore the bullying, parents should take steps to track down the cyberbullies and report them to the appropriate authorities, before taking their child to a psychiatrist who can rebuild their self-worth. The process may be long and frustrating, depending on the extent of the damage, but the effort will be worth it.

Examples of Cyberstalking

The news is filled with stories which prove that cyberbullying is a very real threat and it does n0t discriminate.

The Case of Gabriela Green – In January 2018, two 12-year-old girls were accused of leading another girl to commit suicide due to their cyberstalking. Gabriela Green was found unresponsive in her home and pronounced dead on arrival at hospital. During the investigation, her family and friends revealed that she had been a victim of cyberbullying. While an investigation into her social media accounts and text messages revealed the culprits, it could not bring her back from the dead or give her family closure. The accused girls revealed that their aim was to create trouble between Gabriela and another child via baseless rumours, like the fact she had an STD. They also made threats to spread her personal information online. The bullying included vulgar and derogatory comments which an adult, let alone a pre-teen, would have had difficulty brushing off.

One of the accused also revealed that he had encouraged her to take her life after a failed suicide attempt, when she had called him. What makes this story tragic is that the accused are minors who will have to live with the gut piercing guilt and shame of what they did for the rest of their natural lives.

The Case of Kenneth Weishuhn – In April 2012, 14-year-old Kenneth Weishuhn died by suicide a few months after coming out as gay. The boys in his class bullied him mercilessly over his sexuality and even created a hate group on Facebook that targeted him, and people like him.

When he was asked about the bullying, Kenneth, like most victims of bullying, would just brush it off and say he was fine.

They took their bullying to the next level by adding his friends to the group and by giving him death threats on his cell phone. The bullying was merciless, persistent, and aggressive to the point that it became too much for the tortured boy and he hanged himself in his family's garage where he was found the next morning.

The Case of Rebecca Ann Sedwick – In September 2013, Rebecca Ann Sedwick, a 12-year-old student, died by suicide by jumping off a silo tower. She had a difficult life and been diagnosed with depression and anxiety before the bullying started. After switching schools, she started receiving anonymous messages via ASKfm, a site that allowed users to send anonymous questions to their friends.

When she started receiving messages that asked her to take her own life and claimed that nobody cared about her, Rebecca started getting suicidal thoughts. The bullying only grew worse, which eventually led to her suicide.

The Case of Amanda Todd – Sometimes, even asking for help does not get victims the help they need. Take Amanda Todd, for instance, who died by suicide in October 2012. The 15-year-old took her own life by hanging herself when she could not take the cyberbullying anymore and her appeals for help fell on deaf ears.

Prior to her death, she had posted a YouTube video in which she used a series of flashcards to describe her terrible ordeal and how she was being blackmailed to expose herself on webcam. A blackmailer had convinced her to send him a topless photo of herself and then later threatened to spread it online if she didn't give him a 'good show' later. The abuser continued to bully and blackmail her and even spread the picture all over social media, which only drove her to her tragic decision.

The Case of Brandy Vela – In November 2016, Brandy Vela turned a shotgun on herself after cyberbullying pushed her over the edge. The 18-year-old received abusive messages for months from bullies who had used untraceable phones to keep her in their sights so to speak. Someone had even gone so far as to create a fake Facebook page to target her.

The harassment was mostly focused on her weight, but some of the bullies actually went so far as to place her pictures on online dating sites with false information, like the fact that she was willing to have sex for free.

Even after changing her phone, the bullies found

her and continued their assault, which eventually led her to take her own life in front of horrified and helpless family members. The fact that they could not convince her to drop the gun no matter how much they pleaded points to the mental anguish she felt that blocked sense in lieu of pain.

The Case of Grace McComas – In March 2012, Grace McComas took her own life after a friend raped her and then threatened her when she revealed what he had done. The bright and active teenager was raped under the influence of Oxycontin, a drug that dulls the senses. Grace testified in court against the perpetrator and the cyberbullying began. She was called derogatory names and told that she should just kill herself multiple times. A tweet also said that she should have her fingers cut off because she was a snitch. She tried to get help from local authorities, but the 'help' was largely unhelpful and unable to prevent the tragic outcome.

The fact is that children, especially teenagers, do not realise the extent of their actions and often find out too late that social media can be a trap. Young people do not know how their words really affect their victims. In their minds, they are just having a good time teasing a friend or fellow student. In the cases above, the victims just wanted the mental torture to stop because reality was just too painful. Parents and caregivers are responsible for ensuring that they equip their children with various gadgets. This ought to include putting monitoring apps in the children's phones to observe and control what sites the young ones go to. By setting limits and monitoring their internet activity, parents can go a long way towards preventing other parents from suffering in the same way they did.

The ever-changing digital world has made teen life drastically different from the analogue era. Today, bullying is not just restricted to the playground or the classroom. It gets into our bedrooms via social media and websites that encourage and entice young minds to think and act in ways that only make them doubt their own self-worth.

Chapter 10

THE ENTERTAINMENT INDUSTRY

In my opinion, there is not enough conversation around the mental well-being of artists and those working in the entertainment industry. It is not sufficiently acknowledged that footballers, entertainers, actors, and singers face an incredibly unique challenge that involves an extremely high level of uncertainty, anxiety and stress. They face the burden of being the object of delight and pleasure for thousands or millions of fans. The pressure they face is immense compared to other professions. This includes the pressure to be creative, satisfy the cravings of the fans and always being on top.

They also must maintain a perfect public image of themselves, keep in perfect shape, and exhibit perfect behaviour, while being in constant competition with others. There is also the pressure of breaking through and being accepted by the crowd. I have often looked at the long queues at the auditioning for programmes such as *Britain's Got Talent*, *The Voice* or the now rested *X Factor*. The queues go on for miles and contestants must line up for days to get a 5-minute spot. There is also the self-doubt and the managing of their feelings when they have been rejected.

Two things stand out with acts in this field; first is 'the show must go on' mentality and the responsibility that they think they have to their fans. Unfortunately, that is a role that no one can live up to, even if they fall sick. Second, there is the pressure of maintaining the pace, which sometimes drives them to use alcohol and drugs to cope. Of course, this comes with the attendant consequence, which can be the development of mental health issues and, sometimes, a mental disorder.

Besides this, there is an additional level of complexity that comes with 'stardom', which makes people believe that celebrities do not suffer because their money and influence mean they will have access to services and medications. However, just because celebrities have amassed fame and fortune does not mean that they are immune to mental health issues.

The conditions the artist works in can be stressful, full of anxiety and gruelling, be it, as an actor, painter, musician, or writer. The workers end up putting in very long hours rehearsing, etc., which often undermine their mental well-being. Before getting their breakthrough into the spotlight, they have to work for free or 'for exposure'. Maintaining a healthy sense of self can be difficult if your work, passion, and skills are consistently devalued in this way.

Currently, there is not much research or support out there for artists or a spotlight on the problems they face. Undiagnosed mental health disorders, anxiety, depression, and substance abuse are common mental health issues that plague the entertainment industry. It is recognised that some professions are high-stress jobs; however, the entertainment industry has witnessed a remarkably high level of performers who abuse substances and a very high number of suicides.

Many entertainers have taken their own lives.

The question I ask is, why is there a high rate of suicide among celebrities even though they are portrayed in the media as being super happy people who have it all together?

In 2016, the Centre of Research of Excellence in Suicide Prevention (CRESP) was established by the Australian Government to implement a coordinated and multifaceted intervention strategy to detect people at risk of suicide earlier and conduct research aimed at understanding and reducing suicide rates. They posited in one of their researches that, "Hollywood directors and producers need to step up to the plate and provide their actors with the emotional support that is clearly needed to survive the doomed trajectory of their career path."

For example, in South Korea, there have been several entertainment celebrity suicides in the past several years. In 2009, following a spate of several 'cluster suicides', a study was commissioned to find out the link between these incidents and some celebrities' suicides. The study looked at the pattern following the suicide of seven celebrities and established a link. It reported that there was a significant increase in the risk of suicide during those times when the celebrities took their own lives. There were similarities in the pattern of the deaths and an increase in suicides by people with characteristics that matched those of the celebrities, such as the same sex, age, and method.

Actors

There are some quotes below from some actors that may make us understand the pressure they face and the thinking of some of the stars in the entertainment industry. It appears that sometimes artists get enmeshed in the characters that they play, and this may be an escape for them from what hides behind the smoke and mirrors of fame. Perhaps the roles that actors play can reflect their own self.

Quotes

"With any part you play, there is a certain amount of yourself in it. There has to be, otherwise it's just not acting. It's lying." - **Johnny Depp**

"Acting is not about being someone different it's finding the similarity in what is apparently different, then finding myself in there." - **Meryl Streep**

"Process takes many forms. But really, we're talking about intentions – what we need and what we want in that

moment. Just give yourself something different each take and see what happens." - **Brad Pitt**

"Acting is all about honesty. If you can fake that, you've got it made." - **George Burns**

"One thing about acting is it allows you to live other people's lives without having to pay the price." - **Robert De Niro**

Contrary to some belief, celebrities do not get treatment and medication for free. They end up paying an arm and a leg for private rehab facilities so they can heal without being harassed by fans that placed them there in the first place! They are stars first and individuals second; individuals who suffer from the same addictions that others do. They just need the privacy to heal, which they never get.

What celebrities fail to realise is that, even if they do check into rehab, it does not mean they will miraculously get better. Rehabilitation is just the first step on their journey to recovery, like anyone else who suffers from addiction. What makes their experience particularly harrowing is that they are faced with the same disruptions and circumstances that placed them there in the first place.

That is why a number of celebs relapse a couple of weeks after getting out of rehab – their newly healed brain is not allowed the rest it needs to recover fully when it has to contend with tours, television appearances or new film roles. The pressure is relentless because, unlike a regular employee, they cannot call in a temp to take their place for a while as they recuperate. They are the only ones who can do their job because their fans expect to see and hear them.

In the entertainment industry, the artist or star is just one element in a brand that makes up an entire business. However, if this crucial element collapses, so does the business behind it, as fans leave in droves by diverting their attention to the next kid in the block. Something as simple as scandalous paparazzi pictures or a gig cancellation can snowball into a PR nightmare, and the star rarely comes out of it unscathed.

That is because when fans see such images or see a celeb fall from grace, they lose sympathy for them. What they are really doing is peeping into someone's private life and refusing to relate to it. The image that a celebrity wraps around himself or herself is misleading so that fans do not realise what they are going through to entertain them. They realise that no one wants to know they are suffering from depression, anxiety, or even bipolar disorder because a celebrity is what their fans want them to be.

No addict wants to keep using the substances that made them addicts in the first place. So, what if a star suffers from substance abuse? They hear the same relentless voice in their head that regular addicts hear, which keeps telling them they are not good enough, and they turn to medication to silence it. This gives them a brief but welcoming respite from those voices, but the emphasis is on 'brief' – when the medication wears off, the voices come back stronger than ever, leading to a vicious cycle of substance abuse that turns into addiction.

Most celebrities hide their pain because they fear losing the only source of income they have. On the other hand, they are doing themselves a disservice because they are only masking their condition to please fans, which only makes it worse. The only way they can heal fully is by putting their life on hold – a life that does not have a pause button. Here are some celebrities who finally revealed what life is like on the other end of that spotlight:

Tarai P Henson

The *Empire* star revealed in a 2019 interview that she suffered from depression and crippling anxiety which kept getting worse by the day. The fact that she was not given time to deal with her issues made her spiral out of control to the point that she had to hire a therapist. However, that move helped her in ways that her friends could not. The therapist gave her the truth which hurt, something her loved ones were never able to tell her for fear of hurting her.

Big Sean

The prominent rapper, Big Sean recently spoke up about his struggles with mental health in a March interview. He revealed that he felt disconnected from the world and the people around him and had a hard time feeling good about himself. To heal, the rapper admitted that he had had to take a step back so that he could find himself again. That was when he started going to therapy and got in touch with his spiritual side. This allowed him to regain clarity and think about the people he allowed around him and to influence him in the industry and in his personal life.

Justin Bieber

The child singer turned superstar opened about his struggle with trust issues in a recent interview that he took part in with his wife, Haley Baldwin. He revealed that he would get really depressed during tours and was still a long way from getting through his issues. He also visited several doctors to try and take care of his personal issues which included therapists. Besides depression, Bieber also suffers from anxiety, but refrained from taking medication that could have made him an addict – a brave decision from a celeb who rarely got time to relax and shut down from tour to tour.

Mel Gibson

Before he ever won an Oscar, the *Braveheart* star, Mel Gibson was making headlines for all the wrong reasons owing to his struggle with bipolar disorder. He was infamous for his on-set pranks and after-hours partying. When he got help, he was diagnosed with manic depression.

David Harbour
David Harbour of *Stranger Things* fame recently revealed in a podcast that he was forced to check-in at an asylum when he was 25 years of age after being diagnosed with bipolar disorder. In the podcast, he admitted that self-care was especially important in the industry, not what others recommended. He admitted that well-wishers advised him to take up yoga and meditate and stick to a healthy diet and reduce his smoking habit. However, he insisted that no one could heal him except himself and that he needed his own brand of self-help to heal personally.

Mariah Carey
Mariah Carey was diagnosed with bipolar disorder back in 2001 but she only opened up about the experience 17 years later in 2018. That is how long it took her to get to a place where she could work without her mind rebelling against her. Her reason for speaking up about her disorder was to unveil the myths behind mental health and reveal how isolating it can be for sufferers, whether they are in the spotlight or not. She also opined that the condition does not have to define who you are and

when we realise that, we can control it rather than allow it to take over.

Selena Gomez

Selena Gomez was quite candid about her struggles with mental health and she openly revealed that she had had to step away from the spotlight for a while to take care of hers. This was back in 2016 when she had been forced to cancel mid-tour, so that she could get treatment for her anxiety and depression. After she came back, she addressed the issue at the American Music Awards where she reminded viewers that they did not have to suffer alone and encouraged them to get treatment as soon as possible. She recently stepped away from her social media accounts for the same reason and had no qualms about doing it either.

Chapter 11

MENTAL HEALTH AND SPIRITUALITY

Spirituality and mental health – the link between these two areas of life is not often recognised. In fact, on the face of it, you would not think there was any link between spirituality and mental illness/well-being or psychiatry.

But we are becoming increasingly aware of the ways in which some aspects of spirituality can offer real benefits for mental health. One of the essential protective factors in achieving balanced mental health is our values and beliefs. Our values and beliefs are reflections of culture, spiritual experiences, and customs.

Our sense of spirituality is often heightened during times of bereavement, negatives change, emotional stress, loss or terminal illness.

The study of the mind and psychiatry is recognising to a great extent the role of spirituality, religion, values and beliefs in prevention, early intervention, and recovery from mental illness.

What Is Spirituality?

Spirituality is the ability to connect with the Supreme Being or Divinity. Spirituality. This means different things for different people, but it has these common characteristics:

- It is a source of our beliefs and values
- It provides a strong sense of cultural identity and associated language, food, and/or traditions.
- It is a religious faith of any kind, whether or not it is practised as part of a specific faith community.
- It helps us find happiness, meaning and purpose in our life. An awareness of beauty or a sense of strength gained from nature or the arts.
- A devotion, contemplation, or meditation, whether as part of a religious practice or not, regardless of where it happens.
- It can make us hopeful and give us strength at times when we feel the world is against us.
- It provides strong familial or community bonds

between you and others, including friends, family, or the wider community, so that you feel you have something to offer that others need and value

• It guides us in seeking relationships that heal us and allows us to get in touch with our own needs.

All these experiences are part of the human condition and they are just as important for people who suffer from mental illnesses and intellectual disabilities. They are just as effective for them as they are to so-called 'mentally healthy' individuals who may or may not be hiding their own suffering.

While traditional healthcare practices can relieve physical pain, they often overlook the mental scars that are left behind long after an illness or injury has done its damage. Spirituality emphasises the healing process and this is not just to alleviate the disease that made it necessary. It helps us to understand our place in the world and how our experiences can help us deal with our pain by seeing it as part of the journey we call life. In other words, it helps us to mature, learn and develop in ways that physical healthcare falls short of. After all, if we cannot be free of our demons way after our physical wounds have healed, those wounds will still continue to haunt us.

Spirituality vs. Religion

There is a difference between spirituality and religion. A person can be religious and not spiritual and vice versa. Spirituality is not necessarily tied to any religious belief or tradition. Although culture and beliefs can play a part in spirituality, every person has their own unique experience of spirituality – it can be a personal experience for anyone, with or without a religious belief.

Contrary to popular belief, spirituality and religion do not go hand in hand. While certain religious traditions do involve individual and universal spirituality, the fact that each type has its own worshipping traditions, sacred texts, beliefs, and traditions creates barriers that block intrinsic healing. Spirituality does not tie itself down to a specific religious doctrine or tradition because it is part of every religion in one way or the other.

Belief systems and culture are part of it insomuch as they affect each of us individually. Every single person has his/her own experiences that shaped them and their outlook on life. Spirituality allows us to connect with ourselves and to other people irrespective of their religion. In other words, it can be a personal experience for anyone whether they are religious or not.

The Role of Spirituality
– A barrier or an aid to Mental well-being?

Mental health illness/disorder/conditions don't discriminate, and they take no prisoners. Those who suffer from them want a space where they can feel safe and secure from the voices in their head and even from loved ones who do not understand their unique needs. They also want to be treated with dignity and respect and feel they are valued and have a place in the world just like anybody else. The traditional view of the Psychiatrist was that the causes and treatment of mental illness have three dimensions:

• the biological;
• the psychological;
• and the social.

Hefti in his book, *Integrating religion and*

spirituality into mental health care, psychiatry and psychotherapy, advocated that a fourth dimension should be added, **the spiritual**. ,He posited that this dimension should be taken seriously as a significant factor in resilience and recovery.

The Birmingham and Solihull Mental Health NHS Foundation Trust (BSMHFT) recognises that: *"'Spiritual care' has emerged as the way in which we facilitate and empower people to identify their spiritual needs and find ways of meeting these. has been working hard to develop and deliver high quality, evidence-based spiritual care."*

The patient needs time; privacy and a place where they can worship in peace and receive encouragement that can help them develop their faith. They also want to be forgiven for past transgressions with prayer and reflection.

In acknowledgement of the role that spirituality plays in recovery, The Royal College of Psychiatrist (RCP) founded The Spirituality and Psychiatry Special Interest Group (SPSIG) to provide a forum for psychiatrists to explore the spiritual challenges presented by psychiatric illness, and how best to respond to patients' spiritual concerns.

RCP noted that more than 50% of patients held a form of spiritual or religious beliefs they saw as important in helping them cope with mental illness, but often felt unable to discuss such concerns with their psychiatrists.

While all religions have a belief system, values and culture at their centre, spirituality is a state that all humans can access or experience irrespective of whether they held a religious belief or not.

That is why spiritual assessments should be part of every mental health assessment process.

It is sometimes difficult to tell the difference between someone's spiritual state and mental health? For example, the Pentecostal Christians believe in speaking in tongues and the Holy Ghost. Some of the experiences that spiritual people explain they go through may appear to be psychotic or delusional expressions to people who don't hold the same values.

It is important to note that mental health and spirituality are linked and the research evidence suggests that religion and spirituality can be both a protective factor and a contributor to mental illness. For some, religion offers support and a sense of meaning, a protective factor against suicide and substance misuse. For others, such involvement seems to make a person vulnerable to mental health problems. Perhaps the spiritual content of many people's mental health problems leads to involvement in spirituality or religion. Perhaps mental illness in general is so threatening to one's sense of self that one is forced to consider spiritual and religious issues.

Certainly, disturbances in the spiritual state and mental illness have many features in common:

- They are intangible, neither can be seen heard or felt directly by another person.
- They are holistic, as both have wide-ranging effects on a person's whole life, thoughts, feelings and behaviour.
- Both can be based on unusual spiritual-type experiences and may include extreme emotion.
- They are individual; every person experiences and interprets them in their own individual way.

When we consider all these factors, it is therefore not surprising that they all interact, and we often cannot distinguish one from the other. We now recognise that mental illness has a spiritual dimension, just as it has biological, psychological and social dimensions. Some service users struggle with spiritual matters, whereas others find great comfort in their religion or spirituality. The nature and importance of the spiritual dimension will thus be unique to each person, in the same way as the other dimensions. Our recent research, validating our new recovery scale (SeRvE), confirmed that spiritual ill-being is felt by a significant number of service users. It also showed that spiritual well-being, in general, is highly prized by service users for their recovery.

Spiritual issues are thus especially important for many mental health service users. It is therefore right that they are routinely addressed as part of their mental health care.

It may be argued that where people abuse substances to cope with the symptoms of mental illness, like depression or anxiety, a connection or exploration with spirituality can perhaps help with healing and recovery. For that to be possible, mental health professionals have to determine the difference between a spiritual crisis and mental ailment, particularly when they seem inseparable.

A good way that mental health professionals can do this is by asking patients whether they would categorise the pain they are going through as religious or spiritual. It would also help if they were asked what it is that makes them hopeful about the future or what are the things that keep them going during difficult times?

The answers to such questions usually reveal the patients' main spiritual concerns as well as the methods they use to cope with their internal struggles. Some other questions that a mental health professional could ask to get a holistic overview of their charges include:

• What support can your family and the community you live in give to you?
• What strengths and knowledge do you have that you think should be encouraged?

Of course, the best way to get detailed and insightful answers is to slow down the spiritual therapy and to be as gentle as possible. Exploring spiritual issues can be a therapeutic process since it already deals with inner strength and the experiences that make us who we are.

For that to be possible, the past, present and future should all be delved into. For instance, unexplained emotional stress is often the result of past trauma due to bereavement, abuse, or a major loss. Asking how those incidents have affected them can unravel years of emotional blockades that a person has set up to protect him or herself. After those knots have been loosened, they can then be asked to focus on the present by redirecting their focus on themselves with questions such as:

- Do you feel respected by the people around you?
- Do you feel valued?
- Are you able to communicate with others freely and clearly without shutting down?
- Do you think that there is a spiritual aspect to your current suffering? If yes, would including a spiritual leader from your community provide help?
- What should be understood about your religious beliefs that can help your healing process?

After getting answers to these questions mental health professionals can then focus on the person's future by asking them what they feel it holds for them in keeping with the replies they gave. Are they willing to discuss it more? Do they have fears for their future? Do they feel they need to be forgiven about anything and by anyone?

The next step should be to determine what kind of support can work for them, what can be done to get them the help they need, who should be their secondary caregiver and who can explore their spiritual concerns.

Spiritual Healing Practices

Spiritual practices span from the religious to the non-religious, but irrespective of the path they take, people who suffer from mental health issues can find answers to several of the abovementioned questions through them. They can do that by:

- Taking part in a faith or religious practice, such as services or charity work.
- Going on a religious retreat.
- Spending time in the great outdoors reconnecting

with nature and with themselves.

- Spending time meditating, or in reflection or in prayer.
- Listening to sacred music, hymns, psalms and religious positive affirmations.
- Spending time reading religious texts or literature.
- Joining sports teams that involve trust and cooperation.
- Exploring their creative side through painting, gardening, etc.
- Maintaining and repairing family relations.

The fact is that spiritual practices can help us develop parts of our psyche and personality that can rot with disuse and lead to mental health issues as a result. They can help us become more mindful, persistent, honest, kind, calm, hopeful and compassionate towards our fellow man. They do this by helping us to:

- Be more honest with ourselves and see others the way we want to be perceived.
- Remain focused on the present, as well as alert and attentive.
- Relax and maintain a peaceful state of mind.
- Develop empathy for others and disregard faults.

- Forgive others quickly for the sake of our own mental and spiritual well-being.
- Help others who are suffering, without expecting anything in return.
- Judge when we should speak and act, and when we should remain silent.
- Give without feeling drained or losing hope.
- Grieve without losing our sense of self.
- Realise when to let go of past hurts.

The bottom line is that spirituality helps us to get peace of mind by emphasising our personal connections and our connection with the world around us. It does this via reciprocity which helps us realise that when we help others, we are also helping ourselves.

Today, mental health professionals have to develop a spiritual side of their practice if they wish to remain committed to the people they have to guide and heal. That is the best way to create a healing cycle – those who are healed spiritually often aid others who are going through the same thing as they did.

Religion and Spiritual Counselling

Contrary to popular belief you don't have to be religious to benefit from spiritual counselling. This type of therapy is available to anyone who wishes to avail themselves of it, and can even benefit those who don't follow a particular religion or don't identify themselves as religious. In fact, you can also consult a spiritual counsellor who follows a completely different religion than your own or has beliefs that are contrary to yours.

So how can someone who does not follow a religion benefit from this type of therapy? That is the beauty of this therapy, it can be used to help people figure out whether they are religious or spiritual. It can give clarity to beliefs and help a person to understand how they can use religious beliefs to bring their life back into balance.

If your spiritual counsellor is also a licensed health professional, then he or she has to adhere to certain ethical standards that all medical practitioners have to abide by. In other words, they cannot force their beliefs onto you – rather, they should guide you towards a path that is defined by your personal spiritual needs during the therapy.

Spiritual Counselling vs. Psychotherapy

Spiritual therapy is different from psychotherapy because the latter does not delve into religious issues and topics. In fact, it is frowned upon, according to psychoanalytic theories, and the therapist also cannot reveal his or her religious and spiritual persuasions to their clients, including personal information. Spiritual counsellors, on the other hand, delve deeply into religious topics since it is central to their treatment.

This is understandable as the spiritual therapist has to make personal connections in order to encourage someone to share their spiritual beliefs or retain some for that matter, which is only possible if they reveal their own religious or spiritual inclinations.

Unlike psychotherapy, spiritual counselling sessions do not follow standard protocols or stages. They play out differently for different people, depending on how fast they heal and what their own beliefs are. The way the therapy proceeds also depends on needs for the process as per their religious background.

Certain sectarian counsellors may use specific religious practices during therapy sessions. For instance, if both the counsellor and the client are Christian, the counsellor may try to make a connection by reciting from scriptures. Non-sectarian counsellors, on the other hand, may draw from meditative practices, such as yoga.

What Can Spiritual Counselling Help With?

As mentioned before, spiritual counselling can help people deal with a wide range of disorders and mental health concerns, especially those who suffer from depression and anxiety.

It has also been known to treat schizophrenia as well as help people through the 7 stages of grief after the loss of a loved one. It can also help people overcome substance abuse and even addictions, such as alcoholism.

In fact, the AA 12-step program for treating alcoholics is based on religious principles. The 12 steps repeatedly refer to God and those who seek this therapy have to admit they are powerless and that only a higher power can save them. This involves a moral inventory that encourages them to admit their faults, open themselves to God so that those faults can be removed, as well as make amends with people they have hurt due to their addiction, and reconnect with God through meditation and prayer. They are also encouraged to spread the word about the programme and encourage other alcoholics or substance abusers to seek spiritual healing from the programme just as they did.

However, the 12 steps that make up the programme of recovery are neither a statement nor a belief. They simply describe what the founding members did to get sober and stay away from addictive substances that had ruined their life. If you think about it, this spiritual therapy does not heal with new ideas. All you have to do is be open to healing, stop denying your faults – especially those that made you turn to the bottle in the first place – confess to someone who is not invested in you emotionally or personally and turn to prayer or meditation to self-heal.

That is exactly the course of action that spiritual movements have advocated throughout the world for decades. All the steps do is frame those principles for alcoholics who are too sick, angry and frightened to drag themselves out of the hole they have dug themselves into.

The steps provide a simple step-by-step procedure that compels alcoholics to admit they have a problem. To do that they first have to admit that: the drink has beaten them, they must clean themselves up, they have faults and they must do what it takes to bring their life back on track. This includes maintaining a relationship with anyone who can keep them sober and working with other alcoholics to help them walk the same healing path. In other words, with spiritual therapy such as the AA 12 step program, those with mental health issues can feel useful again with personal growth.

What You Should Look for In a Spiritual Counsellor

Before seeking a spiritual counsellor, who can help you find your way to a healing path, make sure that, besides having religious affiliations, the one you choose is also a registered healthcare professional. The BAME community gives a lot of respect and reverential positioning to religious leaders who are usually the first point of call when there is a crisis.

The common practice is that the Pastors, Priest, and Imams are expected to intercede on the behalf of the congregant to God ask for a reprieve from whatever is ailing them. There have been several cases of religious leaders who are not trained psychologists or psychiatrists offering advice to their follower that what ails them is spiritual and the result of demonic possession, and they can only get relief when the demon is cast out. It is therefore especially important that whilst seeking a spiritual counsellor, the person must be given ethically sound support and their needs are prioritised during the therapy.

Although seeking a spiritual counsellor who shares the same beliefs is preferable for most people, it is not a necessity for healing. You just need to find one you are comfortable with opening up to. The stronger your bond with the therapist, the faster you can heal and see positive results.

To narrow down your choices, ask the spiritual therapists who you have looked up the following questions:

• Are you certified as a spiritual counsellor? If so, which boards are you registered with?

- Do you have a licence as a mental health professional?
- What are your religious beliefs and inclinations?
- Will the fact that we have different religious beliefs matter during the therapy?
- Do you see yourself as sectarian or non-sectarian?
- How will you help me spiritually?
- What are your rates and how long will the treatment take?
- How often will the sessions take place?

Keep in mind that most of the answers will only be revealed during a session or multiple sessions. After all, how can any therapist determine the time a client will take to heal? It will depend on your past experiences, traumas and what the therapist must do to make you come to terms with the issues that are causing your mental breakdown.

Avoiding Spiritual Abuse

The answers to the questions asked earlier can also help you avoid so-called spiritual therapists who may try to manipulate others via religious beliefs. This is spiritual abuse, pure and simple, and it is not easy to recognise. It can have negative and long-lasting effects that could exacerbate your mental health issues rather than heal them. This is commonly seen in families and/or romantic relations with a partner who is in a cult of sorts.

So how do you realise that you are being spiritually abused? If the therapist is shaming you into 'behaving' or to making you act in a certain way, it is a key sign. If you are shamed for your beliefs, either by their words or their actions, are not allowed to practice your beliefs or are being controlled as a result of the 'spiritual healing', you may be a victim of spiritual abuse.

One other sign of spiritual abuse to look out for is single-minded thinking. If your parents or a spiritual leader discourage you from questioning their spiritual practices and punish you when you show doubt or they are not willing to discuss a difference of opinion, you are being abused.

Some other classic signs include the following:

- Using spiritual belief or faith to extort money for certain services and goods.
- Insulting your personal and spiritual beliefs.
- Forcing you to make a choice that compromises

your spiritual and religious inclinations.
* Forcing you to limit your choices.
* Forbidding you from discussing the 'instructions' he gives you with others.

With the right spiritual therapist or even a suitable sectarian therapist, people who suffered from spiritual abuse can get their life and perspectives back on track.

Remember, like any other form of therapy, spiritual counselling also has the potential to be unethical. For instance, it would be unethical for a priest that you have known for years to become your therapist. This is completely against the practice since a therapist should not know a client from any other context as it would affect the results they get.

Additionally, a spiritual counsellor has to respect your beliefs without pressuring you into adopting ones that he/she thinks can bring you 'salvation.' That can result in an ethical dilemma since it will create a conflict between their religious beliefs and duties and their responsibilities as licensed health practitioners. To ensure this does not happen, the counsellor has to ensure that they always prioritise their client's best interests.

Chapter 12
CONCLUSION

Mental health issues are not matters to joke about. If the illness impacts a person's quality of life and affects their ability to live a 'normal' life, it becomes a disability. Undiagnosed mental illness is an unseen, silent killer that takes no prisoners and does more damage to a person's self-worth than any amount of physical abuse ever can.

This book has looked at the various barriers that are precluding people from early intervention and how we can pull these barriers down.

We have looked at the various factors that causing the barriers. There is a dire need for us in the community to understand what mental illness is. We cannot deal with what we do not know. That is the reason I have written about some common mental illness.

Please do always remember that your port of call should be your doctor. Refrain from self diagnosing however; be aware of the signs so you can seek for help when needed.

The Mental Health First Aid Training is a good way to round up your training. Attend accredited mental health awareness trainings, seminars and conferences.

Offer a listening ear, be genuine about your care for people and please do not keep quite about issues when they become overwhelming.

We can break the barrier. We can change the perspective about mental illness and create a better world for people to recover where there is no stigma or judgement against them.

So what are you waiting for? Break the barriers that you have set up around yourself and take that helping hand or seek it.

The power to heal lies within us.

REFERENCES

Office for National Statistics (11 December 2012) Ethnicity and National Identity in England and Wales: 2011. Available at:

https://www.ons.gov.uk/peoplepopulationandco mmunity/culturalidentity/ethnicity/articles/ethn icityandnationalidentityinenglandandwales/2012-12-11

https://www.psychologytoday.com/us/blog/bri ck-brick/201405/the-stigma-mental-illness-is-making-us-sicker

National Institute for Mental Health in England. (2003). Inside Outside: Improving Mental Health Services for Black and Minority Ethnic Communities in England, London, Department of Health

Taylor, C. (2016). Review of the youth justice

system in England and Wales. Ministry of Justice. Retrieved from: https://www.yjlc.uk/wp-content/uploads/2016/12/Review-of-the-Youth-Justice-System.pdf

https://www.psychologytoday.com/us/blog/brick-brick/201405/the-stigma-mental-illness-is-making-us-sicker

http://thenationshealth.aphapublications.org/content/45/1/1.3

https://books.google.com.pk/books?id=gmCxeAw7Z4C&printsec=frontcover&dq=mental+health+and+stigma&hl=en&sa=X&ved=0ahUKEwjC1MzQ8oLfAhWM6Y8KHSodDugQ6AEIJTAA#v=onepage&q=mental%20health%20and%20stigma&f=false

https://ps.psychiatryonline.org/doi/pdf/10.1176/appi.ps.55.2.185

https://books.google.com.pk/books?id=mf6MIScKn0EC&printsec=frontcover&dq=mental+health+and+stigma&hl=en&sa=X&ved=0ahUKEwixnpO-x4PfAhXDXisKHYWwAbAQ6AEISDAG#v=onepage&q=mental%20health%20and%20stigma&f=false

https://digital.nhs.uk/data-and-information/publications/statistical/adult-psychiatric-morbidity-survey/adult-psychiatric-morbidity-survey-survey-of-mental-health-and-wellbeing-england-2014

https://ontario.cmha.ca/wp-content/files/2012/07/olm_stigma_matters_200902.pdf

http://www.pacifichealthsummit.org/downloads/2012_Summit/PHS12_MentalHealth.pdf

http://ontario.cmha.ca/wp-content/files/2012/07/moods_media_200812.pdf
https://fullfact.org/health/nhs-spending-mental-health/

https://onlinelibrary.wiley.com/doi/pdf/10.1002/jpoc.21080

https://www.mentalhealth.org.uk/a-to-z/b/black-asian-and-minority-ethnic-bame-communities

http://www.irishhealth.com/article.html?id=9002
https://www.ncbi.nlm.nih.gov/pmc/articles/PMC3858464/

http://diversityhealthcare.imedpub.com/irish-people-and-mental-health.php?aid=2144

https://thriveglobal.com/stories/mental-health-black-community/

https://books.google.com.pk/books?id=3EwrDw AAQBAJ&printsec=frontcover&dq=mental+health +in+british+asians&hl=en&sa=X&ved=0ahUKEwi ssuao5cnfAhWCKQKHZMICqoQ6AEIJTAA#v=o nepage&q=mental%20health%20in%20british%20a sians&f=false

https://www.rcpsych.ac.uk/docs/default-source/members/sigs/spirituality-spsig/spirituality-handbook-of-spiritual-care-in-mental-illness.pdf

https://www.nice.org.uk/guidance/cg123/evide nce/cg123-common-mental-health-disorders-full-guideline3

https://www.ncbi.nlm.nih.gov/pmc/articles/PM C2738337/

https://www.barebiology.com/pages/guide-omega-3-fish-oil-for-brain-health

https://www.barebiology.com/blogs/news/how

-omega-3-physically-affects-childrens-brains

https://www.psychologytoday.com/us/blog/yo
ur-brain-food/201109/balancing-your-fat-intake-
controls-depression

https://psychcentral.com/blog/does-social-
media-cause-depression/

https://www.medicaldaily.com/3-easy-ways-
avoid-effects-social-media-depression-420745

https://www.socialmediatoday.com/marketing/
how-much-time-do-people-spend-social-media-
infographic

http://endofcyberspace.com/health/effects-
cyberbullying

https://www.verywellfamily.com/what-are-the-
effects-of-cyberbullying-460558

https://www.usmagazine.com/celebrity-
news/pictures/stars-whove-battled-mental-
health-issues-2013136/big-sean/

https://www.glamourmagazine.co.uk/gallery/ce
lebrities-talking-about-depression-anxiety-and-
mental-health

https://www.who.int/whr/2001/media_centre/
press_release/en/

https://www.mentalhealth.org.uk/sites/default/
files/impact-spirituality.pdf

https://www.ncbi.nlm.nih.gov/pmc/articles/PM
C2755140/

https://www.thrivetalk.com/spiritual-
counseling/

https://www.nhs.uk/conditions/antisocial-
personality-disorder/

Curtis, S. Health and Inequality: Geographical
Perspectives. Sage: London, (2004)

Walter, B. Mapping Irish Health and the 2001
census. Anglia Polytechnic: Cambridge, (2004).

Davies J. Exploring The Mental Health Experiences
of the Irish Community in Wirral; University of
Leeds, School of Geography, University of Leeds,
(2005)

Bracken, P, Greenslade, L, Griffin, B and Smyth,
M. Mental Health and Ethnicity: an Irish

dimension. The British Journal of Psychiatry, 172, (1998).

Gibbons F.X., O'Hara R.E., Stock M.L., et al. (2012) The erosive effects of racism: reduced self-control mediates the relation between perceived racial discrimination and substance use in African American adolescents. Journal of Personality and Social Psychology, 102(5), 1089-104.

Williams D.R. & Williams-Morris R. (2000) Racism and mental health: the African American experience. Ethnicity & Health, 5(3-4), 243-68.

Bhui K., Nazroo J., Francis J. et al. (2018) The impact of racism on mental health. Available at: https://synergicollaborativecentre.co.uk/wp-content/uploads/2017/11/The-impact-of-racism-on-mental-health-briefing-paper-1.pdf

Wallace S., Nazroo J. & Becares, L. (2016) Cumulative Effect of Racial Discrimination on the Mental Health of Ethnic Minorities in the United Kingdom. American Journal of Public Health 106(7), 1294-300.

Jang S., Sung J., Park J., Jeon W., Copycat Suicide Induced by Entertainment Celebrity Suicides in

South Korea Psychiatric Investigation. 2016 Jan; 13(1): 74–81.

Powell A. (22 May 2019) Unemployment by ethnic background, Briefing Paper Number 6385. Available at :http://researchbriefings.files.parliament.uk/docu ments/SN06385/SN06385.pdf [Retrieved 18/06/19].

Barnard H. & Turner C. (May 2011) Poverty and ethnicity: A review of evidence. Available at: https://www.jrf.org.uk/sites/default/files/jrf/m igrated/files/poverty-ethnicity-evidence-summary.pdf [Retrieved 18/06/19].

Joseph Rowntree Foundation (2017) UK Poverty 2017: a comprehensive analysis of poverty trends and figures. Available at: https://www.jrf.org.uk/sites/default/files/jrf/fil es-research/uk_poverty_2017.pdf [Retrieved 18/06/2019].

Lammy, (2017). The Lammy Review. An independent review into the treatment of, and outcomes for, Black, Asian and Minority Ethnic individuals in the Criminal Justice System. Retrieved from: https://assets.publishing.service.gov.uk/governm

ent/uploads/system/uploads/attachment_data/
file/643001/lammy-review-final-report.pdf

White, C. (2016). Incarcerating youth with mental
health problems: A focus on the intersection of
race, ethnicity, and mental illness. Youth Violence
and Juvenile Justice, 14(4), 426-447.
https://doi.org/10.1177/1541204015609965

Taylor, C. (2016). Review of the youth justice
system in England and Wales. Ministry of Justice.
Retrieved from: https://www.yjlc.uk/wp-
content/uploads/2016/12/Review-of-the-Youth-
Justice-System.pdf

https://www.local.gov.uk - Being mindful of
mental health The role of local government in
mental health and wellbeing

Borras L, Mohr S, Gillieron C, Brandt P-Y et al
(2006) Religion and spirituality: How clinicians in
Quebec and Geneva cope with the issue when
faced with patients suffering from chronic
psychosis. Community Mental Health Journal 46,
77-86

Introducing The Nous Organisation

Mission:
To raise awareness about mental health issues among the Black, Asians and Minority Ethnic (BAME) Communities in UK and Africa

Objectives:
- To provide essential information through workshops, open mic sessions and conferences to members of the community about mental health.
- To engage the youth and raise awareness about mental health issues.
- To serve as a bridge between psychiatrists and other professionals in raising awareness about mental health in our communities.
- To campaign about the improvement of services for members of the Black and Minority Ethnic through social media and other local newspapers and outlets.
- To provide advocacy for those who are and were disadvantaged by existing health services.
- To work collaboratively with Local Authorities to implement their mental strategy.
- To offer peer support to parents, careers and persons that may be going through mental health services.

Nous Organisation Convener:
'Lade Hephzibah Olugbemi

Website: www.nousorganisation.com
Email: info@nousorganisation.com
Facebook: TheNous1
Instagram: nousorganisation
Twitter: nousorg

Printed in Poland
by Amazon Fulfillment
Poland Sp. z o.o., Wrocław